D1187499

THE MANDARIN

HONG KONG

THE MANDARIN™*
HONG KONG

Nigel Cameron

THE MANDARIN
HONG KONG

First published 1984
This edition published by the Mandarin Oriental Hotel Group
Hong Kong 1989

MANDARIN ORIENTAL ™*
HONG KONG

ISBN 962-7480-01-0

*® Registered US Patent and Trademark Office and/or in other countries worldwide

Contents

Foreword

When The Mandarin reached the age of maturity at twenty-one, we published a book to celebrate. People, it seems, like to read about the history of a grand hotel, so we have republished the book.

In the past five years, much has happened. The Mandarin is now Mandarin Oriental, Hong Kong, and with The Oriental, Bangkok, one of the two flagship hotels of a Hong Kong publicly listed company, Mandarin Oriental International Limited, that includes some of the finest hotels in the world.

In a changing Hong Kong, Mandarin Oriental has been completely renovated from reception to roof and is poised to enter the nineties, continuing to set the standards that others follow.

With increasing competition, we have put much of our effort into providing a secure and steady working environment for our employees upon whose efforts the hotel's reputation is built. We have been very fortunate to keep so many of our loyal and dedicated staff, and over 100 of them have been with us for more than twenty-five years. It is these men and women who have helped to inspire all the many guests who have joined us in that time and to give them the sense of belonging and the personal, caring service that has made the Mandarin Oriental name a by-word in the world of travel.

While the renovations have replaced some of the fabric of the hotel, the soul and the spirit remain unchanged.

In this book, we look back on the growth of that spirit, and on the staff and the many guests who have helped it grow. We look forward to writing the next chapter in the Mandarin Oriental legend.

Robert E Riley
Managing Director, Mandarin Oriental Hotels Limited

The Start of a Great Venture

On the 7th of July, 1960, the board of The Hongkong Land Investment and Agency Co. Ltd. (as The Hongkong Land Company Ltd was then named), which had been founded seventy-one years previously, decided to proceed with the demolition of one of its oldest buildings in central Hong Kong. This was Queen's Building. The intention was to build in its place what the minutes of that meeting call a 'first-class hotel.'

This was the initial decision which triggered off a chain of events, the first result of which was The Mandarin and, in the ensuing two decades, the rise of several more such hotels in a steady surge of expansion of Hongkong Land's hotel interests which can only be described as phenomenal.

The fact that the Company was in the hotel business at all was an accident, the result of a fire which gutted a large portion of the old Hong Kong Hotel on the corner of Pedder Street and Des Voeux Road. Hongkong Land bought the site and, after a couple of years spent in evolving a suitable scheme for redevelopment, began to build a combined office, shop, and residential structure. The intention was to lease this to Hong Kong & Shanghai Hotels Ltd., but negotiations with that company fell through and the Company decided to run the residential floors by itself. The Gloucester Hotel, the Company's first venture into the hotel business, came into being.

The Gloucester outmoded

By the time of the board meeting of July, 1960, The Gloucester was thoroughly outmoded. To the majority of the board the suggestion, which had been given a certain amount of flesh at meetings over several years, that the equally old-fashioned Queen's Building should be replaced by an hotel, appeared as a good, if novel idea. There was, however, some opposition to this innovative scheme by those who, naturally, wanted to redevelop the site as an office and shop structure. The decision to build an hotel instead was largely the result of the infectious enthusiasm of the chairman of the board, Hugh Barton, who was the Jardine, Matheson *taipan.* He it was who argued against an office and shop structure in spite of the figures which had been prepared and which demonstrated that the immediate returns would be greater than on an hotel. He was convinced that there was more scope for future expansion in the hotel industry than in office premises which, at that time, seemed to him to be reaching saturation point.

Hotel or office?

Hugh Barton made numerous points at the crucial board meeting — something which he referred to many years later as giving the board 'four or five minutes of Irish blarney.' For him, Hong Kong in 1960 had a higher potential growth value in the foreseeable future as a tourist centre rather than in the industrial and commercial areas. Moreover, he wanted to see a Company diversification into hotel investment with a ratio of 75 per cent offices and 25 per cent hotels, and thought this a 'reasonable proportion.' Offices, he felt, would face more competition than a first class hotel.

In this he was undoubtedly correct for, all over Asia, what had been in pre-war days great hotels such as Raffles in Singapore, The

H.D.M. Barton, CBE, was taipan of Jardine, Matheson & Co. Ltd. from 1955 to 1963, a position which has carried (and still carries) the chairmanship of Hongkong Land since the inception of that firm in the days of Sir Paul Chater. His first taste of the East came when his father was appointed Chinese Counsellor at the British Embassy in Peking. After studying at Cambridge he returned to China in 1933. His grandfather on the maternal side, A.P. McEwan, had been a Jardine's partner around the turn of the century, and his godfather was David Landale's grandfather — Landale later to become a Jardine's taipan. 'Hence,' says Hugh Barton, 'I got my chance to join the old firm when I left Cambridge.'

The sole expatriate vacancy at that time of depressed trade was for a tea taster, and he accepted that. World War II saw him in the Irish Guards, and he spent the final six wartime months as a Lieutenant-Colonel on Lord Louis Mountbatten's staff at Kandy.

The war over, he rejoined Jardine's in Shanghai and became a director in 1946. 'After eight years in the hot seat,' as he puts it, he retired in 1963, not long before The Mandarin opened

Oriental in Bangkok, and The Peninsula over the harbour in Kowloon, were by 1960 hardly comparable in their standards of comfort and food to their counterparts in the West. Apart from Frank Lloyd Wright's Imperial in Tokyo, there was hardly a first class hotel in the Orient.

Given that an hotel was to be built, the Company had the advantage of having a magnificent site of its own, an immediate advantage over its competitors; and, moreover, they were in association with Jardines and with Butterfield and Swire, and through them with the leading airlines and with tourist opportunities of some size.

It took much more than those few minutes of 'blarney' to sway the board. It took in fact considerable courage, for at the time the

The waterfront, Central Victoria, in the early years of the 20th century. Queen's Building is at the left

apparent advantages in quick returns on an office block were obviously attractive.

The decision was made, and what Hugh Barton and the board had done was to take what turned out to be an immensely imaginative step in the semi-dark. But on that step there followed consequences which at the time could hardly have been foreseen by even the most imaginative chairman of any board.

In fact, later, when Hugh Barton was visiting the London office of Jardine, Matheson which had gone public in 1961 with shares 49 times oversubscribed, both John and Tony Keswick were there. Hugh Barton sums up their attitude to the Hongkong Land board decision: 'When they heard this crazy fellow Barton was going to build a luxury hotel they were rather worried. They asked one or two top property men in the City about the project. And *they* said you

never *build* a luxury hotel, you wait for someone else to do that, and when it's gone bust a couple of times — then you buy it.' But by that time they had a board decision. Yet while The Mandarin was building it was often referred to in certain quarters as 'Barton's folly.'

City Hotels Limited

The same board meeting agreed that a separate company should be formed to take control of the hotel segment of Hongkong Land, and this company, City Hotels Limited, was duly floated, its prospectus dated 31st of January, 1961. This prospectus announced the issue at par of 299,680 shares of HK$5 each, to be offered in the first instance to the persons registered at that date as holders of the existing shares of The Hongkong Land Company Ltd. The directors were Hugh

*Queen's Building, graceful forerunner of The Mandarin, with the
Queen Victoria Memorial and statue of the Duke of Connaught*

Barton, Harold Benham, Henry Cleland, Richard Lee, Donovan Benson, Man Wai Lo, and William Knowles. The secretary was Anthony Paul Ross, more familiar as Tony Ross, who set up the company office on the 4th floor of Gloucester Building. T.A.P. Ross was appointed hotel consultant and manager, and City Hotels Limited was incorporated by Messrs. Deacons, solicitors, on the 10th of November 1960.

In this manner there began an enterprise far greater than any of those present at the crucial board meeting could have guessed. Even the wisest heads in the year 1960, could hardly have envisaged the metamorphosis that was to overtake Hong Kong and the East in general in the following two decades. In Hong Kong in particular it has been said that more new building was completed in those twenty years than in any comparable period

in any other city in history. Whether or not this is objective truth, no one who knew the city in the 1950s and who looks down from the plane arriving either from a western or an eastern direction would fail to nod agreement. Vast new towns and vast new industrial constructions extend all over the visible areas of Kowloon and along the coast, from Castle Peak in the west to Leiyuemun in the east, and what was in many a place open green hillside and valley has long been filled with concrete rising up to twenty storeys and more.

Yet in 1960, on the island, the reclamations made around the turn of the century largely at the instigation of one of the founders of Hongkong Land, Sir Paul Chater, terminated at the waterfront which was just over the road from Queen's Building and its neighbour across the green square, The Hong Kong Club (from whose Long Bar on the

The Mandarin rising within its bamboo scaffolding

ground floor it was a common sight to see a sampan tied to a post on the shore).

In the next twenty years the waters of the harbour receded a hundred yards or so, the old dockyard was filled in, the City Hall rose on new land, to be followed later by the tallest building owned by Hongkong Land — Connaught Centre — now accompanied by the new, Exchange Square. Almost every structure owned by the Company in the adjacent areas, together with several owned by others, has been demolished, and a complete

new heart has been constructed in the body of downtown Hong Kong.

During that same time, and highly relevant to a Company with hotels, Hong Kong exports rose from HK$3,831 million in 1963 to HK$83,032 million in 1983. Indicative of the rise in numbers of visitors to Hong Kong, the non-resident arrivals at Kai Tak airport rose from 315,000 in 1963 to 2,775,014 in 1983. And at the same time Hong Kong became the third most important banking centre of the world. In terms of an hotel being required,

Hugh Barton was more right than he knew.

Speaking of those years when he was Jardine *taipan*, he said recently: 'The thing that always amazed me about Hong Kong was that you could do twice as much in the same time as you could in the City of London — for the simple reason that the people you wanted to see were all around you, at most a five minute walk away. That was one of my pressing arguments for building a top-class hotel.'

While today this is still to some extent true — for the financial community certainly — major companies have spread to new developments in Wanchai (rather more than five minutes walk away), the movement largely brought about by the removal of what, in the nineteenth century, was termed 'the constriction at the waist' caused by the army and navy having grabbed strategic land in early days adjacent to each other. Once the docks moved harbourward and the army moved out of Victoria Barracks altogether, the way was open eastward, and construction began and flourished in Wanchai, whose entertainment and Suzie Wong image slowly wilted among the highrise office blocks.

But The Mandarin's position still makes it an extremely convenient hostelry, as Hugh Barton envisaged. And Suzie Wong's address is now on the other side of the harbour.

Building The Mandarin

Leigh and Orange, one of the oldest architectural practices in Hong Kong, first set up in business in 1874, was a natural choice for the new Company, City Hotels Ltd., to make in choosing the designer of their new hotel. They had been the architects of Queen's Building, a structure they completed in 1899, which was about to be demolished and its site redeveloped. Furthermore, Leigh and Orange had designed and built the Gloucester Building after the fire of 1926, and had completed it in 1932.

John Howorth, then senior partner in the firm, recalls how somewhat earlier than the board meeting of July, 1960 he had been contacted in relation to possible plans for a new structure on the Queen's Building site. He had in fact, on the board's instructions, prepared two plans, one for a composite shops/offices complex costing HK$21.4 million, and another for a shops/offices/hotel (330 rooms) development costing HK$27.9 million, of which HK$6.5 million was allocated to the hotel section. This second plan called for a vertical division of the building into offices on two sides and hotel rooms on those other two which faced the harbour and eastward toward The Hong Kong Club.

Architect's brief...

'At the July board meeting,' Howorth recalls, 'I was given the brief to build the maximum number of bedrooms for the Queen's Hotel, as it was then called, which could be accommodated within the plot ratio; and of course the sort of public rooms that such an hotel would require. My initial sketches in fact included more public rooms than were eventually built — something that

proved to be a mistake, and was rectified later by constructing more.

'I worked basically with Bevan Field who was general manager of City Hotels Ltd., and with Tony Ross, manager of the Gloucester Hotel and general manager designate of the new hotel. We formed a tight little team and between us worked out the major problems involved. Initial designs took perhaps four to five months to complete, but almost all those ideas had to be modified in the light of discussion of the needs and functions of the hotel as they were envisaged step by step.'

...and problems

Leigh and Orange had a problem. How to increase their staff quickly to cope with this very large commission to build a multi-storey hotel? 'We were putting up the first mechanical-electrical hotel in Hong Kong, probably the first in the Far East.' By sheer luck, Howorth remembers, he had a phone call about this time from a young Australian architect, Frank Eckermann, who was bearing a letter from a mutual acquaintance in London. He at once asked Eckermann if he would abandon the world tour he was on, and join the firm. Eckermann agreed. From then onward the hotel was the joint architectural effort of the two men.

From Company records, and more vividly from the memories of the people most involved in the day-to-day problems of construction, a picture of its progress can be put together. Two other men were intimately involved from the beginning — Vernon Roberts working under Bevan Field, and William F. Powell.

Bill Powell, as he is always known, had

Don Ashton (light jacket), the principal designer of the original Mandarin interiors, became involved largely by accident. His successful career as designer of sets for such films as David Lean's Bridge on the River Kwai, *Peter Ustinov's* Billy Budd, *and Richard Attenborough's* Young Winston *had not led him into hotel interior design until some friends bought the Mayfair hotel in London. They asked him to redesign 50 rooms for the hotel and a couple of new suites. His brief was to make them look like film sets. He carried out this work and that was, so far as he was concerned, the beginning and end of his hotel involvement.*

At the time, Tony Ross, (left), was manager of the Mayfair. That was the link. And since the original Mandarin interiors Don Ashton has been brought in to redesign whenever major alterations were needed. He has forsaken the stage and now works exclusively in hotel design and decoration.

One interesting link with his career as set designer adorns The Mandarin — the splendid gilded figure of Justice, which was the figurehead of the clipper ship in the film Billy Budd, *transported from England, gave the Clipper Lounge its name. Architect John Howorth is at the right*

been on the staff of Hongkong Land since 1956. He was on leave in England when in the summer of 1960 he recieved a letter from Bevan Field saying that on his return he was to be put in charge of the project management of the new hotel venture. This letter followed hard on the heels of a Company announcement published in the *South China Morning Post* on the 9th of July, 1960 that it proposed to demolish Queen's Building and put up a '500-600-room hotel on the site.'

Incredible as it may now seem, the Gloucester Hotel was at that time still regarded as one of the top six in Asia — with

Vernon Roberts

Raffles in Singapore, The Peninsula over the water in Kowloon, The E. & O. in Penang, The Oriental in Bangkok, and The Imperial in Tokyo. All were old and most in rather less than first-class condition, having survived a war after which little had been done to upgrade them.

Action

Returning to Hong Kong in November 1960, Powell recalls being met at the airport by Vernon Roberts in a smart sharkskin suit and a big American car. He started planning at once. The Queen's Building, its four open verandah floors, its slight air of a Moghul palace built in a foreign clime, soon began to tumble in a cloud of dust under the hammers of the demolition contractors. There is a forlorn-looking picture in the *South China Morning Post* of the 3rd of November, 1960, taken from the roof of the adjacent St. George's Building, of the undignified end to a dignified structure that had seen profound changes in Hong Kong's business life and weathered them all with a certain serenity.

By year's end the piling contractors were ready to start on the new foundations. The target date for what the hotel trade calls the 'soft opening' — the opening of the main public rooms and some floors of bedrooms while the rest are still being completed — was set for September 1963, just two years and eight months ahead.

This close scheduling was necessary to save time, and for the same reason it had been decided to let the piling contract *before* demolition of the old building was complete. In practical terms this meant that information on what lay beneath the ground was scanty. To put up a building of 25 storeys it is essential to know what you can stand it on, whether the substructure is capable of bearing the weight of the proposed superstructure. And at that time the extent of piling, and of scheduling of the new substructure for a building immensely more heavy than Queen's Building, were hardly determinable factors.

The load was to be transferred directly through steel piles to the rock strata that had formed the original sea bed before the recla-

Bill Powell

mation long ago. Large pieces of machinery had to be imported from abroad and cylindrical steel piles driven. The first few gave no trouble, the next encountered boulders and, even worse, a rubble mound — remnant of an ancient sea wall. And tidal water moved in and out of the site with fish and other less delectable contents of Hong Kong's even then somewhat polluted harbour. It became obvious that the chosen piling method just wouldn't work without incalculable delay.

More problems

The matter came to a head one Sunday. While withdrawing one of the 60-foot tubes, control was lost and the huge cylinder shot into the air, plunging across the boundary hoarding. Luckily no one was hurt, but the reaction of the Chinese workforce was that something would have to be done to placate what they saw as a very angry dragon.

The piling method was altered, the hotel structure proposed was lightened; and the contract for the substructure was completed almost on schedule. Whereupon the building contractor, Sung Foo Kee, took over and began on the body of the hotel.

Bill Powell, when the Company were opening tenders for the contract, remembers his trepidation about the budget figure for this part of the work. The contract awarded to Sung Foo Kee was within the HK$11.5 million sum — money that today would hardly build eleven modest apartments, and would certainly not pay for a structure such as the hotel to rise above the fourth floor at most. The total cost of the completed and equipped hotel, including a sum of about HK$20 million for the site value, was in the region of HK$80 million. Times have changed . . . .

With a flying start, the concrete frame of the building was up and topped out a year after the general contract started, and by then other contractors — sub-contractors employed directly by Hongkong Land — mechanical, electrical, windows, furniture, fittings, and all interior decor among them — were well advanced. Naturally such a complex operation was not without its problems. Bill

Arriving for The Mandarin topping out ceremony: left to right,
Harold Lee, architect John Howorth, Hugh Barton, and a guest

Powell recalls visiting the site twice daily to clear the bottlenecks.

Suzie Wong intervenes

'This often meant using the site intelligence network to locate the cause of a hold-up in the work. One such blockage was causing serious delays, and I discovered that a rather colourful European character, a site manager to one of the contractors, had lost control because of his fondness for the afternoon company of Hong Kong ladies in the Suzie Wong district of what was then a flourishing Wanchai. After substituting a bright young Chinese who was keen but inexperienced, I eventually re-employed the European play-boy, now reformed, under my direct super-vision and he soon got his workmates to per-form satisfactorily.'

Architect Frank Eckermann of Leigh and Orange, remembers a host of such problems, many stemming from the fact that 'we were

building this new type of mechanical-electrical hotel. At first the extent of the com-plexities was perhaps not wholly understood by the Company, but that was overcome in time. It was all new technology in Hong Kong at that time, but some of the methods employed by Sung Foo Kee were the age-old Chinese ones. Scaffolding was that intricately tied network of bamboo that looks so fragile but is in fact very strong. Outside the facade of the rising hotel there was a sort of ramp zig-zagging up, floor to floor, with nailed-on slats of wood forming footholds. I always refused to use this contraption, never having seen such a thing in my working life pre-viously. So I didn't go above a certain level until the service lift was installed to that height. After working in Europe and North America, it astonished me to see the primitive but effective methods used in Hong Kong.

'One other surprise to one new to Hong Kong was the bunch of amahs who had some

*One of Don Ashton's original colour sketches
for The Mandarin lobby*

sort of concession to cook food on the pre-mises for the workers. I was rather against this because of the potential fire risk. But in the end I had to give in to what was a firmly established local custom.

Fast food

You never knew from day to day which floor these amahs would be cooking on. They brought in all the food and navvied it up that precarious ramp, set up their charcoal cook-ing stoves, cooked, and served around fifty or sixty workers per floor. Then they packed up neatly and left. It was a smart bit of private enterprise, really. I never quite fathomed who organised it. But there was a small woman labourer with a big operatic voice who seemed to be the power behind it. When we eventually had to evict the cooks, since we needed space to get on with the interiors, there was real hell to pay!'

An unusual feature of the design of the public areas was the comparatively low entrance lobby giving, left, up three steps, to a very high-ceilinged sitting area. This in turn was surrounded by what came to be called the Clipper Lounge, reached by a fine, wide, well-proportioned stairway.

'The sitting area,' John Howorth says, 'was designed from the very earliest stages to give the arriving guest the feeling of luxurious use of space,' and this it does achieve. 'The three steps up from the lobby incidentally gave the air-conditioning contractors a useful extra 21 inches in the basement where there is much plant installed. And the Clipper Lounge at first floor level, surrounding a double-height sitting area on ground floor level, did not turn out to be the extravagant use of space it might have seemed. Most of it was built over the coffee shop and the carport. Personally I felt that *visual* aspects were what mattered, but I realised Bevan Field would have a hard time explaining to the board why I wanted to build

*The Seal of the
Grand Secretary*

What's in a Name?

The word mandarin *seems to have entered the English language with Mendoza's* History of China *which was translated by Parke in 1589. According to this theory of the origin of the word, it is derived from Portuguese* mandar, *which in itself stems from Sanscrit* mantrin, *a counsellor.*

While this is quite certainly the first appearance of the word in English, there is a cognate source. It happens that in the hierarchy of the Chinese bureaucracy from ancient times the highest ranking civil servant of the Chinese Empire was always the holder of the title Grand Secretary of the Wen Hua Palace. Wen Hau is the northern Chinese pronunciation of the two characters, which in Cantonese sound as man wah. *Probably there was general confusion among Westerners in the Orient between the sound of* man wah *and* mandar *in Portuguese — merchants from Portugal being by far the earliest Western seaborne traders to southern China.*

It was not long before Mendoza's History *appeared in many European languages, and* mandarin *appears in as many guises. At first it denoted solely the Grand Secretary. Later it came to mean any official in a position of authority with whom traders and others came in contact in Canton and elsewhere.*

Later, with familiarity, the word was taken to mean the Chinese language as spoken by the bureaucrats of China — what is now the official pronunciation and called kuo yu, *the national speech or language.*

But there is yet one more option on how mandarin *arrived in English. The characters* 滿大人 *signify 'Manchu great man', the alien people who were the rulers of the Ching dynasty in China. The pronunciation of those characters in* kuo yu *is* man da ren. *It seems almost too good to be true!*

this area in such a manner. With the cooperation of the air-conditioning people, J. Roger Preston & Partners, I presented the plans as a purely practical solution to *their* problem, pointing out at the same time the change of level between lobby and the sitting area benefitted the design at no extra cost. So all went smoothly with that.'

John Howorth adds: 'When Don Ashton, the interior designer, saw those plans he grasped at once our reasons for planning the double-height area and the change of floor level. And he came up with a brilliant suggestion for covering the tall marble wall with an eye-catching display of gilded Chinese carved panels. It was this design, I think, that secured him the appointment as interior designer of the public spaces in the hotel.'

Interior design

Don Ashton takes up the story. 'One morning in London I had a call from Tony Ross asking me to enter a competition for the design of the interiors for an hotel in Hong Kong of which he was manager designate. And out of the blue the board of City Hotels Ltd. liked my designs, Hugh Barton being particularly enthusiastic.

'Everyone seemed to me, when I arrived in Hong Kong, to be anxious to make a marvellous hotel. I stayed for six months then and we made a prototype room in the Gloucester Hotel. Hugh's wife, Rosie Barton, and their two daughters were the arbiters of taste in what the interiors ought to look like.'

The comparision with the elaborate exercises which are nowadays conducted before arriving at the final 'look' of any area of an hotel tends to put this enthusiastic bit of amateurism (and simple good taste) in the shade. But it seems to have been just that intense interest on the part of all concerned which won through.

Returning, Don Ashton stayed on for 18 months until the interior was completed and the hotel opened.

One curious fact about the building of the hotel is that apart from the slight experience of Don Ashton in redesigning some rooms for the Mayfair in London, none of the 'team' (as Bill Powell and others term the small group responsible for The Mandarin as it finally appeared) had had any previous experience of their roles in the physical and conceptual aspects of a great hotel. Leigh and Orange had indeed built the Gloucester, but long before the days of Howorth and Eckermann, and it was a pre-war concept with little bearing on the new structure. Tony Ross was an experienced hotel manager, but had never participated in the design side. Veron Roberts likewise had managerial experience, but Bevan Field and Bill Powell were newcomers in the hotel arena. The last named remarks on all this: 'I've heard many take credit for the conception of the design of The Mandarin, but to my mind it was this whole team of people, all new to the task, that made The Mandarin what it became.'

What's in a name?

Curiously enough, no one seems to remember when, and by what process of reasoning or suggestion, the structure which was called Queen's Hotel when it began to be built became, long before it was finished, The Mandarin. But the name stuck.

The 'team' held frequent meetings, and

given a forceful character such as Bevan Field, and Tony Ross not used to this style of corporate life, these were not always plain sailing. Given, too, the talents, aspirations, and the differing ideas of the members, it would have been surprising if they had been. 'After our frequent meetings,' Powell relates, 'we would adjourn to the Saddle and Sirloin (the Gloucester Hotel's 'speciality' restaurant) and run through the results of the meeting, and get ourselves sorted out for the next day or week.

Water rationing strikes

'When we were on the last laps of the process, with only a few weeks left before opening date, water rationing in Hong Kong was further restricted. Reservoirs were at dangerously low levels, and we had four hours of water supply every four days. Air-conditioning water and flushing water were obtained from our own supply taken from the sea just over the road, but we still needed large amounts of fresh water for various systems in the hotel. Sea water distillation plant was on order, but not yet here. So we hired tankers and brought in well water from various sources, mostly in the New Territories. And by altering the pipes we used the small swimming pool as a temporary reservoir.'

A further dilemma is recorded by Frank Eckermann. 'Shortly before opening day — a month or so before — it became evident that the English company from whom all the door fittings for the whole hotel had long ago been ordered, had failed to put the order on the right boat. We were faced with the daunting prospect, doubtless it would have been

unique in building history, of an hotel opening its doors but being quite unable to close any one of them! Desperate telephone calls secured from an American manufacturer the necessary door fittings by air freight at huge expense — but at least on time!'

The Mandarin opened its doors to guests on the first day of September, 1963. On the same day the following prudent advertisement appeared in the *South China Morning Post.*

The Gloucester Hotel has pleasure in announcing that the Saddle and Sirloin Grill Room and Bar, the Main Dining Room and Private Rooms, the Lounge and Mexican Bar on the 8th floor will remain open for business. The residential bedrooms will close on 1st September 1963.

At The Mandarin, by the 1st of September, the ground floor public rooms were complete, as was the restaurant on the top floor, but not all the bedrooms were ready. This was the 'soft opening,' the point of which is that at least the hotel begins to show a cash flow.

'Space-age engineering'

The South China Morning Post also carried an article on the same day about the opening. 'The Mandarin, a new luxury hotel in the heart of Hong Kong, opened quietly today' to receive the guests of the Gloucester 'which ends thirty years of service to the Colony. Only a small proportion of the 650-room 27-storey hotel (actually 25-storey plus a machine-room on top of that) will be in use . . . .' But Mr. T.A.P. Ross promised that all services would be ready in a few weeks. The article enthused about the new standard of

*Advertising the opening of the hotel on the 25th October, 1963
in the South China Morning Post*

elegance and comfort, 'the space-age engineering' by which, from the mezzanine floor 'one is literally catapulted by gentle lifts which negotiate the distance in 21 seconds' — right to the top!

The ground floor and some other floors of rooms being in use, Frank Eckermann relates how, soon after this opening, he was in one of the lifts on his way to the top to have lunch. 'With me were two immaculately coiffured and gowned American women engaged in animated conversation. The lifts were programmed not to stop at floors where work was still in progress, but by some malfunction of the system this one did. The doors opened to reveal the spectacle of two strong Hakka women workers bearing buckets of hot pitch on shoulder poles — and determined to join us and go up a floor or two. The look on the faces of the Americans may be imagined,

before I managed to thwart these determined workers!'

Floral hitch

The night before the formal opening on the 25th of October, Don Ashton recalls how he, with Tony Ross, Vernon Roberts, and Bill Powell all went quite early to dinner at the house of Oleg Perezypkin, a Ukrainian of aristocratic birth who kept a hospitable house and was, incidentally, the supplier of all the table silver to The Mandarin.

'We all came back to The Mandarin after midnight, perhaps not as sober as we had left it,' Don Ashton remembers. 'I think I was just dropping the others off, but anyway I was still standing on the pavement and Tony Ross had gone into the hotel — when suddenly he came rushing out shouting: "Don! Don! You don't know *what* they've done to our hotel!'

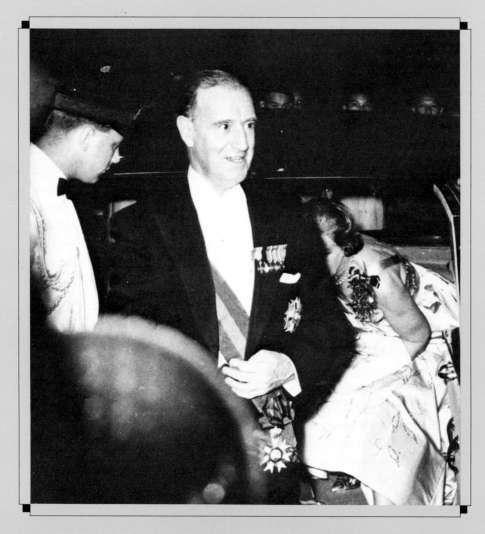

*His Excellency the governor, Sir Robert Black,
and Lady Black arrive for the Red Cross Ball*

'I rushed in with him. And there it all was. The whole place a sprouting mass of *ikebana*. There were lopsided tree-trunks, orchids, dried leaves sticking out everywhere.! They had even hung the stuff on the gold Chinese carvings on the wall! I can't tell you what a mess it looked!

'Vernon Roberts, who didn't mince words, said some unprintable things to the effect that it should all be made swiftly to vanish. So we all set to with some help from the staff, and by about 2:30am. the clean-up was complete, and we went off to bed.'

Teresa Kwa who was running the public relations department, recalls that it was all a mistake on the part of someone who had been offered flower arrangements by the local *ikebana* society, and who probably caught on to the word 'flowers' and didn't know what *ikebana* was. Hence the lightning strike by the flower arrangers. She made peace with the ladies committee the following day.

Grand opening

By opening day, all the rooms were ready for use, and all facilities except the coffee shop (The Causette which was to be supplanted two decades afterward by the new Coffee Shop) were operational. A half-page advertisement in the *South China Morning Post* on the morning of the 25th announced the event with an artist's impression of the main entrance to the hotel where three young couples in smart fashions of that time are seen mounting the steps. One of the men appears to be wearing a dinner jacket, while one of the girls is wearing a hat. It must therefore be inferred that the artist was not familiar with Western sartorial customs, according to which men do not wear dinner jackets for lunch, nor is it *de rigueur* for ladies to put on hats at dinner. Only tiaras will do.

Listing the many facilities of the hotel, the caption suggests that there could be 'no better way to spend either Christmas, New Year, or more especially Chinese New Year, than as guests of The Mandarin Hotel.' The suggestion is commonplace in Hong Kong nowadays, but this may be the first time such a course was proposed.

The Red Cross Centenary Ball of the 25th September, with which The Mandarin opened, in several ways set the tone and the quality of much of the hotel's future activities and of its position in the life of Hong Kong. Sir Robert Black, governor of Hong Kong, was present with Lady Black who was president of the Hong Kong Red Cross Society. Their Royal Highnesses the Duke and Duchess of Kent were there too as guests at a private party. The evening, as reported in the newspapers of the following day, went smoothly and was voted a tremendous success. And not a twig of *ikebana* was in sight.

Retrospect

Far back in the last decade of the 19th century when Sir Paul Chater finally won the long campaign and gained government permission to make the reclamation in Central Hong Kong, thus providing the land on which Queen's Building rose in 1899, he could not have foreseen the tumultuous turn of events that were to combine since then to fabricate the Hong Kong of the 1960s. But he saw a few steps ahead of his time and his contemporaries, and he lived to see the first row of waterfront buildings on the new Connaught Road rise to fulfill their then modern functions.

In something of the same manner The Mandarin, as it was conceived by Hugh Barton with the support of the board of The Hongkong Land Company Ltd was also a product of seeing a little ahead of the times, of guessing intuitively but with fair accuracy and some courage, at the potentials of the near future, of a new period in the world of commercial, industrial, and tourist aspects as they might soon affect Hong Kong.

And The Mandarin was the tangible beginning of a new enterprise — one which Sir Paul would certainly have been excited about — the chain of *grande luxe* and first class hotels in southeast Asia which came later under the wing of Mandarin International Hotels Ltd. Sir Paul would certainly have been proud of them.

*The Mandarin seen from a balcony of the now
demolished Hong Kong Club*

Establishing a Reputation — Ross and Stafford

Just four years after the opening of The Mandarin the hotel was cited by *Fortune* magazine, in the issue of November 1967, among the eleven 'great' hotels of the world.

Failing to discover even *one* great hotel in the Americas, the magazine went on to list those elsewhere on which it bestowed its accolade: the Vier Jahreszeiten in Hamburg; The Mandarin in Hong Kong; Claridge's and The Connaught in London; The Grand Hotel in Rome; The Grand Hotel in Taipei; The Imperial in Vienna; and The Dolder Grand in Zurich.

Among this august group of mature, even in some cases grand duchess hotels, The Mandarin was a mere stripling — but as it turned out a highly precocious one.

In calling its choices 'the great hotels — imperturbable oases in a glamourous world,' a typically swinging sixties manner of stating the case, *Fortune* went on to spell out its definition of the terms. 'A great hotel must be ready for everything, it is not enough that most rooms are faultless; all of them must be, in service as well as in decor and furnishings. It is not enough that the food and wine are impeccable; they must also be served impeccably, even when the restaurant is unexpectedly crowded.'

Any hotelier will agree with the good sense of such statements. But there is a lot more to running a luxury hotel than can be conveyed in statements about those two areas of hotel management alone.

T.A.P. Ross

Tony Ross, The Mandarin's first general manager, would surely have been the first to go along with this. He had been on the spot long before the structure of the hotel was complete. He had assisted in important ways in modifying its design, in equipping and making more workable an hotel which was, with the possible exception of the just-opened Okura Hotel in Tokyo (a much smaller hotel at that time) the sole convincingly *grande luxe* hotel in all Asia in 1963. From that starting point it was then up to him to begin building a reputation for the hotel which would match the unusual excellence of its structure and amenities. The fine quality of an hotel, perhaps more so than in any other business, and like that of internationally famed beauties, may well have been built in at birth; but it has to be assiduously cultivated thereafter.

For a man who was, in the words of one of his secretaries, Vera Slater, 'a very private person, not at all gregarious, a generous and kind host, but rather shy,' the task must have looked a hard one. Running an hotel requires in its general manager considerable contact with the guests. Tony Ross, however, did realise 'that public relations with the guests was a necessary evil, and important enough to let others get on with most of it. He did some entertaining — lunches in the Grill — but always wanted a PR girl or myself to be present. Without being publicly demonstrative about it, he was very concerned for his staff. When we had riots in Hong Kong in the late sixties, and rice was temporarily short and expensive, he ordered that The Mandarin should supply one big bag of rice to each of the staff once a month. And he was right in this — the staff were basically much more interested in the price and availability of rice than in Chairman Mao's little *Red Books*!

'You could always depend on the kind and

Thomas Anthony Paul Ross was forty-two when he arrived in Hong Kong to supervise the establishment of The Mandarin as it rose from the ground meshed in the usual Hong Kong network of bamboo scaffolding. His education had been at Lansing College from which he went on to the University of Heidelberg, and after that to graduate at the Ecole Hotellière in Lausanne. He worked at Claridge's in London before moving to the Mayfair where he was general manager. After a stint there he went on to the Waldorf Astoria in New York, the Boca Raton Club in Florida, and the Mid-Ocean Club in Bermuda.

Of himself he said: 'I come from a family of hotel owners. I waitered in Berlin, studied the kitchen in Paris, and worked the cellar in England.' It was with this solid background of experience from the ground — even the basement — upward, that he reached The Mandarin

caring aspects of him being there. Some of the staff were a little afraid of him. I wasn't — perhaps because I knew some of his problems. I did have one set-to with him — it was during one of Hong Kong's direct hit typhoons. I failed to turn up for work. He was really mad at me, although I told him all public transport had been withdrawn from where I lived. In the end he sent The Mandarin Rolls Royce to pick me up, and he was still fuming when I got to the office. However, he calmed down, dictated a five-line memo to the food and beverage manager on the deplorable quality of the Vichyssoise he had taken the previous evening at dinner. Thereupon, after typing out the memo, I was sent home again in the Rolls!'

Vera Slater sees the vital clue to his character in quite simple terms. 'His real love was

Harold Lee

The Mandarin.' Her handover report to her successor in the job illuminates Tony Ross's meticulous approach to running the hotel — the almost finnicky order that had to be maintained on his desk with every object placed in precisely the same location every day, the necessity to retype telexes and cables in 'proper English' before he would read them, his way of spending very much of his time around the 'back of house,' the need to check the list of what any of his regular guests at teatime preferred to eat.

In those days the Legislative Council of Hong Kong met for luncheon in The Mandarin on the second Friday of each month, the governor or his deputy usually attending. Tony Ross's assiduous attentions to such local functions as this — most of the council members being well known, well-connected, and influential people — probably did a great deal to establish the firm ground of important local patronage for the hotel.

His relationship with Harold Lee, chairman of the board (who lived in the hotel) was particularly close and friendly, and the eminence of Harold Lee was assuredly yet one more factor in spreading the word internationally about the quality of the new hotel.

There emerges from such reminiscences, and from other facts about Tony Ross, a picture of a man exceedingly competent in the management of an hotel; dedicated to that. But also the image of a man determined as a matter of policy to delegate whatever could reasonably and effectively be delegated to his staff. It is obvious that his was not a very visible presence in the public areas of the hotel, equally apparent that he preferred to spend the bulk of his time either at his desk or, with more emphasis, 'back of the house.' This was a style of management that stood in sharp contrast to that of his successor.

Tony Ross died comparatively young, aged 52, toward the end of September 1969, knowing for the last few months that he would not live, yet for the most part carrying out his duties as before. On his death, City Hotels Ltd. took some considerable time to discover a suitable successor — tribute enough to the quality of his management and to the position The Mandarin had attained as a result of it.

Peter Stafford

The man eventually chosen for the job, Peter Stafford, takes up the story. 'In 1963, when The Mandarin opened, there was a tremendous stir in the hotel world — at first because it was such a good-looking place and possibly the best of all the modern hotels of that time. I heard about it while I was assistant general manager of the Savoy Hotel in London. Then in 1964, when I was going to Australia (where I was born) for a holiday, on the way out I decided I'd go to look at this great new hotel. The resident manager at the time was the ex-night manager from the Savoy, and there were three others on the staff who came from the Savoy too — Josephine Law, the housekeeper, Luigi Gambardella, the reception manager, and Hudson who was head porter. I decided not to stay at The Mandarin. I suppose I was far too shy. I stayed at The Peninsula instead. But of course Hudson found out that I was there and told Peter Gautschi of that hotel that they had the assistant general manager of the Savoy staying with them. I went over to The Mandarin and had a look. Peter Costelloe, the resident manager, kindly showed me round, and Tony Ross asked me to lunch.

'And I had a number of friends in Hong Kong, and they took me to The Mandarin for dinner several times. Each time I was impressed. I *loved* The Mandarin.

'Then I went off on my holiday, and then back to the Savoy. That was in 1964. By 1969, I decided as I was the oldest assistant general manager in the world, I would resign from the Savoy. I decided to go back home and discover whether I wanted to be an Australian or a European.

'When I was in Australia, staying with my father, I had a cable from a Savoy client, a man called Ambrose Congreve, who told me that Harold Lee who was chairman of City Hotels was looking for a replacement for poor Tony Ross who had died some months previously. Ambrose was in Bombay at the time, so I sent him my father's telephone number, and said I'd like to know about the job quite soon — I'd already applied for a job in Australia. Mr. Lee rang me next day and I told him I would have to know within a couple of weeks. But he replied that would be difficult as there wasn't a board meeting until February, and it was then January. He said he didn't think it would be possible. I replied that I was sorry he'd wasted his phone call, but that I had booked myself already on a plane for the next day, and I'd also had my cholera injections. Harold Lee said: "You sound the most dreadful bully! I look forward to seeing you."

Challenges

'Well, Harold Lee and I started what was to be a great friendship. He was a splendid — I thought, a wonderful — man with great style and a great knowledge of the world. When he was interviewing me in Hong Kong, he

Peter Stafford began as general manager at The Mandarin in February 1970. Born in Brisbane in 1925, he was educated at St. Laurence's College, and thereafter at the Teacher's Training College. By that time the Second World War was in its latter phases and he joined the Royal Australian Air Force in 1943. This took him to England at the close of the war as a navigator. On demobilisation, he had made up his mind to go into the hotel trade. He began in a small way in the Marine Hotel in the Scottish seaside resort of North Berwick, but his career took him onward to the Palais d'Orsay in Paris, and later to the Baur au Lac in Zurich, and a time in reception at Claridge's in London. In 1954 his long association with the Savoy in London began. He joined that hotel as assistant manager and went on to become assistant general manager, a position which he retained until joining The Mandarin

remarked: "You know, Peter, I've never worked in an hotel but I've learned an awful lot about them because I've always stayed in the best."

'So it was all arranged.'

Looking back on that time, a time of decision that comes to many of us in life when another, or a new, a more exciting or fulfilling choice must be made, Peter Stafford says: 'A job without challenges is not a job. In hotel-keeping every day has its crises, and in a sense one careless remark can ruin a guest's other-wise perfect stay. What you want to do, *must* do as an hotelier, is to provide your guests with a home in your hotel, one to which they will want to return again and again.'

The philosophy of hotel-keeping is something high on the agenda of Peter Stafford's priorities. Not just the thousand details of how a great hotel must be organised, but what sort of impression it will make on the travel-ler, the sojourner, the man, the woman whose life takes him and her round the world and — necessarily — through the portals, the recep-

*Luigi Gambardella, left, exchanging a joke with Ian Hunter,
Director of the Hong Kong Arts Festival, 1972. They
had met before in Amalfi, Gambardella's home town, in 1946*

tions, the dining rooms, the bedrooms, the bars, the totality of service of the world's pre-eminent hotels. To be excellent among the excellent is Peter Stafford's aim, one which he shared with The Mandarin, and one which later on was to be shared with its sister hotels around Southeast Asia.

'One of the great lessons taught me at the Savoy, by a man who was general manager there for my first six years, was this: "If anything is working," he said, "think twenty times before you change it."

'Well, The Mandarin *was* working rather well. It would have been presumptuous of me to have thought I could change anything for the better in the first couple of months there. I spent a good *six* months before I did very much alteration.

'The Savoy taught me another lesson — that was caring for clients. And at The Mandarin I found this extraordinary staff, not only heads of departments but the whole 1,200 of them. The great joy in working with Chinese staff is that they have a tremendous

dignity in giving service. They don't think it's beneath them to look after people. And besides that they have an innate sense of hospitality.'

Peter Stafford says that perhaps what he did in terms of that staff and of the running of the hotel in general was to give the staff confidence in themselves. His approach was to get to know as many of them as possible. He started off by hiring ferries on six Saturday afternoons and asking those who wanted to go on boat picnics, bringing their families along. 'I think it was then they decided I wasn't a bad old *gweilo!* Actually it was moving for me — I'm an emotional man.'

The Mandarin was very fortunate in its staff in yet another way, for many of them who had come over from the Gloucester were still working in The Mandarin and formed a big nucleus of very experienced people. And despite the rather small size of the Gloucester and the greater size and complexity of The Mandarin, 'they weathered the move with little problem, as I understand it, under the aegis of Tony Ross,' says Peter Stafford, paying a graceful compliment to his predecessor. 'The room boys at the Mandarin, as well as all the rest of the staff, had quickly to become more sophisticated. Unlike the Gloucester, we had *linen* sheets. I introduced towels of the finest quality, locally made, and larger than the former ones. I put bath robes in all the suites. These were just a few of the details that required increasing sophistication in the work of staff.'

All hotels require constant renewal of their interior fabric and furnishing, and there are times, regularly recurring, when extensive renewals have to be done. 'Soon after I arrived,' Stafford recalls, 'we recarpeted all the corridors, and we had the carpet made locally this time instead of in New Zealand as originally. We also did the same for the Clipper Lounge and the sitting area of the lobby — this one specially woven and hand-carved. New carpets for the suites were designed by Don Ashton and Frank Eckermann, and also made locally.'

Suites

From the first, The Mandarin had several named suites. Naturally one was named after the hotel itself and situated on the top room floor at the other end of the corridor from Harold Lee's office which overlooked the naval base, H.M.S. Tamar. And when Harold Lee retired, this was turned into the Tamar Suite. 'The Navy gave us a plaque from one of their old ships which we put on a desk in the suite. Then we had the Lotus and Magnolia Suites done by Charlotte Horstmann with all the flair for colour and elegance that is hers, together with the Bauhinia Suite (named after

Hong Kong's official emblem, the flower of the Bauhinia tree), and the Pine Suite with which Frank Eckermann helped me. John Howorth did a fine restrained suite, and Theresa Kwa made the colourful Persian Suite.'

Conversation with Peter Stafford about his years at The Mandarin is an experience in which his wide-ranging statements about all aspects of it are interspersed with detailed observations, neat sketches of personalities whether of the chairman, Harold Lee, or of a room boy.

A reflection of the best

'Once Hongkong Land had decided to build the hotel I know they were extremely un-mean about the project. This was Hongkong Land's great virtue, and it paid off handsomely. I imagine The Mandarin has made more money than any hotel of its size. But the Company has continued to spend a lot of money on it. I spent quite a lot in my time, so did Andreas Hofer, and Peter French is doing the same. That's the way it should be.'

Pausing awhile he says: 'An hotel must always be in some ways a reflection of the best things in the city or the country where it is located. I think this is one aspect in which The Mandarin shines. Don Ashton and others have used a lot of local material and Chinese design in the hotel, but never in a chop suey manner — always with extraordinary style. The guests know where they are — in Hong Kong, in the East, in a bedroom or a restaurant in The Mandarin.

'You know, a hotel manager is very possessive about his hotel. It may be a fault, but

Above: H.R.H. Princess Anne is escorted into
The Mandarin by Peter Stafford. Above right:
Mr. David Rockefeller, former chairman of the
Chase Manhattan Bank, seen at a press conference
in the hotel. Right: Producers of the movie Jaws,
David Zanuck and David Brown, drove around
town in The Mandarin's Roll Royce

The Mandarin's Distinguished Guests

The list of distinguished guests whom The Mandarin has welcomed tells a tale of success, of international recognition of its quality in comfort, elegance, cuisine, and — above all — of its service.

In the first few months, members of the Belgian royal family arrived, and so did the Marquis and Marchioness of Blandford. Broadway star Ethel Merman was an early guest, as was Peter O'Toole. Harold Lee's friend Mr. Richard Nixon paid a couple of visits, and the President of South Korea was also a guest. Such famous stars as Cornell Wilde and Isaac Stern, one of the world's great musicians, were to be seen. The Baron Heinrich Tyssen-Bornemisza whose great house with its even greater collection of paintings stands by the shores of Lake Lugano, spent part of his honeymoon in the hotel. The tycoon of newspaper fame, Mr. William Randolph Hearst was among a host of top

Above left: T.R.H. Prince and Princess Alfonso de Bourbon spent part of their honeymoon in The Mandarin. Left: Mr. Henry Kissinger arrives on one of many visits to The Mandarin, greeted by Peter Stafford. Above: Mr. Julian Thompson, Chairman of Sotheby Park Bernet, talks to The Mandarin's carpenter, Mi Wing-kee, who made the copy of an antique rostrum for the sales

executives and international businessmen and financiers who, as the years go by, have made The Mandarin their home in Hong Kong.

During the term of Peter Stafford the same tale continues, with South Africa's diamond king, Mr. Philip Oppenheimer, Mr. Henry Luce III, the publisher of Time, financier Mr. David Rockefeller, and Pierre Trudeau, then Prime Minister of Canada. The stars of stage and screen and the concert hall are all represented in numbers, and among the royal families of the world, the late Shah of Iran and his wife, and the Queen Mother of Thailand were welcomed.

The Mandarin also welcomed the first of many viewings and auctions of fine Chinese ceramics held by the world's best known auctioneers, Sotheby Parke Bernet, which brought a new dimension to the Hong Kong cultural scene somehow unless he is possessive, I don't think that the hotel has individuality. So my thoughts on The Mandarin are coloured by that care for the hotel and its staff. Both Tony Ross and Hongkong Land realised they had a winner, and Tony Ross was as possessive as I was — even in his time it was selected as one of a few top hotels round the world. I think The Mandarin went from strength to strength with that great staff. And I think, too, that in the course of time one of the things we all learned at The Mandarin was a little humility.'

Asked to explain this, Peter Stafford says: 'The hotel was very full in 1970 — it was the year of Expo in Japan — and we had an extraordinarily high occupancy. We got a bit cocksure, we got a bit too grand. And when we realised this on the management side, we started going round saying "Thank you for staying with us," even when we were 100 percent occupied. Some of the staff looked a bit amazed at this.

'But I had heard, previously — something that made me *shrink* with shame — the reverse: "Oh, you're lucky to get a room!" I think we all learned the lesson. After all, the guests pay our wages. And in fact it's very un-Chinese to say people are lucky to get a room. It's not polite.'

A good buy

Before the opening of The Mandarin, Hugh Barton had arranged that bookings internationally should be handled by Inter-continental Hotels, and this gave the hotel a fine start. They trained the food and beverage staff, they assisted with costing, both in the time of Tony Ross and in Peter Stafford's too. 'If we ever needed help from the best advisors

we hired the best through them,' Stafford says. 'We made use of the Pan American computerised system of bookings, and they did all our marketing and sales for us. This built up an enormous international business, so we have a lot to thank Inter-continental for.

'But of course when we started on our own chain of hotels we were setting up in opposition to them, so we had to pull out. This was when it was decided to join people I knew from my Savoy days, Hotel Representative Inc. — now renamed The Leading Hotels of the World. The Mandarin was their first associate member. And this proved to be of inestimable help to the hotel. Instead of being the most expensive hotel on the Inter-continental list — they used to say we were the jewel in their crown! — we became the cheapest of the HRI list. In fact we were *such* a good buy at that time that this helped us to get our rates up a little.'

VIP connections

Another factor in enlarging and widening the reputation of The Mandarin was, according to Peter Stafford, the enthusiasm of Harold Lee. 'He was so well known internationally. When he went to the States he invariably had a talk with the Pesident — it happened to be Nixon at that time, and whatever subsequently we may think of Nixon, it is indisputable that he was the architect of China-U.S. rapprochement.

'Harold knew everyone, people helpful to the hotel, the US ambassador to China, the head of CBS, people in the British government. He was given a government lunch at Lancaster House in London. Harold was a sophisticated man, a man who attracted peo-

The Morning After

'I used to come down to the lobby most days before eight o'clock — it gave me a chance to see a lot of guests. As I got out of the lift on this particular day,' Peter Stafford recalls, 'one guest said to me: "Mr. Stafford, I'm never going to stay in The Mandarin again." I replied: But Mr. Brown I'm dreadfully sorry. Why ever not? Mr. Brown said: "Well, last night I was not allowed by your night manager to take a friend of mine up to my room."

'What time was this? — "Two o'clock in the morning."

'Well, Mr. Brown I'm very sorry but I'm afraid my night manager obeys my instructions. It was late. One never knows .... We're only trying to look after you. I'm sorry to have upset you. Now, can I help — would you like me to book you a room in another hotel?

'As he was talking to me, my assistant came over and said that a Mr. Smith, a guest, would like to see me.

' "He's awfully cross with us, I'm afraid," he added. "He took a girl up to his room last night and he's been robbed."

'I said: Mr. Brown! Come over and meet Mr. Smith, and when you two have decided what I should do, I'd delighted if you'd tell me!

'And they both roared with laughter and went off and had a very early drink!'

ple from all over the world. Formerly he was old China's representative at the League of Nations, and lived for years in the Georges V in Paris, spoke good French from his education in Switzerland. We needed an ambassador like that for the hotel. But besides all that he was extremely proud of being Chinese, and he gave to The Mandarin just that extra sense of great style.

'Henry Keswick, first as a director and later as chairman of City Hotels Ltd., had his own enthusiasm for The Mandarin. I remember once when we were having lunch I was surprised that he knew so many of the staff by name. And when David Newbigging took over as chairman, he too was very concerned for The Mandarin, rightly so, since it was the flagship of an enormous investment. He recognised also that it is the staff in large part

that makes and maintains the reputation of an hotel.'

Talking of the 'Mandarin family' feeling among the staff, Peter Stafford recalls his worst typhoon in Hong Kong.

'I was having dinner in the Grill with Australian guests when suddenly all the lights went out. We'd been in the midst of this typhoon for hours, so it was hardly surprising. The rain was apparently driving horizontally into the lift motor room on the top of the building and it was flooded. All lifts except the emergency one were out. While the guests went to bed, all the staff used to sleep in the hotel on such occasions, often on the floor, for there was no other place for them. The chief engineer came to me and said they'd have to get a big heavy tarpaulin up to the floor where the motor room is to stop the

Head chef Leung Zi

gap where the water was coming in. They took this up by the sole service lift working and navvied it manually from there upward. When I got up there and they saw my anxious face, many of them gave me a little pat on the shoulder in passing, as if to say "Don't worry, we can cope." I felt then how lucky I was to be working with such people.'

Imperial Banquet

Another time when Peter Stafford felt the staff rallying round in a more than ordinary way was for the memorable Chinese Imperial Banquet. 'I was asked by Gault and Millau, who are the foremost food and hotel critics in the world, to put on a three-day Imperial Banquet at The Mandarin. The reason I tackled this at all was to demonstrate that Hong Kong in this particular line had something worth showing to the world; and luckily, as it turned out, we did.' The Mandarin's Man Wah restaurant had only been in existence since 1967, and had

been managed by C.T. Wu who had joined the hotel as assistant to the general manager in 1964, in the time of Tony Ross. He later became deputy general manager under Peter Stafford. He particularly recalls Leung Zi, the head chef in the Man Wah kitchen. 'We all called him Uncle Zi. In spite of his age and his authoritative standing in the field of Chinese cooking, Uncle Zi was always modest and willing to listen to opinions from others, and always ready to cooperate. It was this attitude of his that greatly assisted the progress of the restaurant.'

Peter Stafford, faced with setting up an Imperial Banquet, confesses: "When I had the cable asking me to do it, I had hardly any idea what an Imperial Banquet was. When I asked my deputy, C.T. Wu, and Lau Man-hon the purchasing manager, and the wonderful old chef Leung Zi, they practically fainted away. They said, no, they wouldn't do it. I replied that I thought I hadn't asked them to jump an

The menu of the Imperial Banquet

impossible hurdle, and would they go away and think about it, and then come back to me tomorrow and tell they *would* do it. I said that I'd give them all the backing in the world, and that I appreciated it would be a hard job. Lau said to me: "Mr. Stafford, if we should fail, we will really have to leave Hong Kong." They all meant that. The disgrace of not bringing it off superbly would be too much.

'They came back next day. Lau Man-hon said: "We'll do it. But it'll cost you!" The price looked like US$25,000, which was a lot in those days.'

An Imperial Banquet consisted of several days feasting on the choicest of foods offered to a Chinese emperor by the provincial governor and mandarins while he was visiting on a tour of the countryside.

Success

'When the first day of the banquet came, everyone was on tenterhooks. Everything had been done to make it as perfect as could possibly be. And we'd all learned a lot about what precisely constituted an Imperial Banquet. And then the guests arrived — two tables of twelve — the first lunch began. Harold Lee was there, and I had asked several local people, Sir Kenneth Fung Ping-fan and his wife, and Q.W. Lee who was well known in Hong Kong as a great gourmet. And there were the world's culinary and hotel press — Naomi Barry from Gourmet magazine arrived only two minutes before we sat down. Most of the guests had come in after long flights and were quite tired. Somehow at first the curtain didn't quite go up as we had hoped, there wasn't the atmosphere of a flourish that there ought to have been. All of us at the end of the lunch were a bit flat, Harold Lee among us. Then just as the guests were all saying their thanks and taking their leave, Q.W. Lee came up to me and said: "Peter, that was the best meal I have ever had. Can I bring

Esther (his wife) tonight?"

'I could hardly answer! Q.W. Lee kept the best table in all Hong Kong! I went into the kitchen where it had all been cooked, to find the chef, the head waiter, and the boys having a bit of a post mortem and looking a little down in the mouth about it. I said: We've done it! Q.W. Lee wants to come back tonight and bring his wife!

We had the most astonishing coverage in the international press. It was a triumph for Andy Hofer of food and beverage, and for the whole staff.

'Christian Millau, I've been told, was having dinner in Paris in June, 1983 when he was asked what was the best meal he had ever eaten. After all that time — twelve years — he replied: "My

three-day banquet at The Mandarin." '

Summing up his time at The Mandarin, Peter Stafford pronounced a couple of sentences which he himself calls 'Staffordisms.'

'The Chinese have no sense that to serve people is beneath them in any way. They're right. Two of the world's most prominent public servants are the Pope and the Queen of England.'

Then: 'Keeping an hotel is really a matter of extremely good manners — and the Chinese have that.'

Keeping an hotel is surely, as Peter Stafford well knows, a lot more than that, but, *au fond*, he is quite right.

Without the good manners the rest is pointless.

Hongkong Land and Mandarin International Hotels Ltd.

When The Mandarin was built and running it does not seem to have been the policy of City Hotels Ltd. to enter any further into the hotel business. But the question of a two-phase development of land formerly occupied by the Jardine's godown at Causeway Bay was the triggering factor that eventually led to expansion in that direction. The development comprised The Excelsior Hotel and the adjacent Convention Centre, in both of which projects Hongkong Land and City Hotels had small investments. The Excelsior was managed by Trusthouse Forte but did poorly, and the management was eventually taken over in 1976 by Mandarin International Hotels for an initial 10-year period.

This meant that the Company added 951 first class rooms to The Mandarin's 544 deluxe rooms.

New horizons

Prior to this, Hongkong Land had been introduced to Giorgio Berlingieri of Italthai in Bangkok through the good offices of the Hongkong & Shanghai Banking Corporation, and in a remarkably short time had entered into an agreement by which it took up 49 per cent of the equity in The Oriental Hotel. With this further addition to its hotel capacity, the Company was in an obviously expansionist mood, and Mandarin International Hotels Ltd. was founded in February 1974.

About this time the Company had its eye on another site which seemed ripe for development, this one in Manila in the fast-growing commercial and banking area of Makati. In early 1975 board approval was obtained to build a multi-storey deluxe hotel of 474 rooms of which The Manila Mandarin Inc. is the owning company with Filipino interests taking up at least 60 percent of the equity. Mandarin International Hotels has a ten-year contract with option to renew for a further ten years.

Another element in the Company's expansion followed on a remark in a board meeting in mid-1973 by the chairman, Henry Keswick, who suggested that there was a very good site in Jakarta. Negotiations with P.T. Jaya Agung were successfully completed, and The Jakarta Mandarin was finished in 1979 with 455 deluxe rooms on 28 levels.

The Royal Orchid

Before the completion of The Jakarta Mandarin, a site scarcely 500 metres distant from The Oriental on the Chao Phya River in Bangkok became available. The old pillared Hongkong & Shanghai Banking Corporation's premises had stood there in all their white stucco and pillared glory for many a bygone banking day. With demolition, the temptation to take up the (at that time) sole available site suited to hotel development right on the river was extreme. In September 1978 the board succumbed to it and approved the project for a multi-storey first class hotel to be known as The Royal Orchid. The owning company is Italthai International Hotel Ltd., and Hongkong Land has a 15 percent equity, with Mandarin International Hotels in possession of the management contract. The Royal Orchid was opened in June 1983 by Her Majesty Queen Sirikit of Thailand.

Another unbeatable location presented in Macau within sight of the jetfoils and hydro-

The Mandarin's Sister Hotels

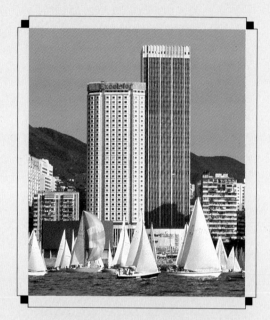

The Excelsior, Hong Kong

The Royal Garden, Hong Kong

The Macau Excelsior

The Oriental, Bangkok

The Royal Orchid, Bangkok

The Manila Mandarin

The Jakarta Mandarin

The Vancouver Mandarin

foils arriving from Hong Kong — and this was taken up by the board of Hongkong Land in May, 1979, and the Hotel opened in mid 1984. Hongkong Land has a 50 percent equity in The Macau Excelsior, and Mandarin International Hotels has the management contract for 25 years with the option of a further similar period.

A marketing service agreement for The Royal Garden Hotel in Kowloon was signed in November 1979, and a further step in expansion was taken in February, 1980 when the decision was made to build in Singapore a 527-room deluxe hotel to be called The Oriental. Hongkong Land took a 15 percent equity and Mandarin International Hotels has the management rights for 20 years from opening date, scheduled for late 1985.

Farther afield

A first venture outside the Southeast Asian area was begun by a board decision of August 1981 when it was agreed to take up a 51 percent equity in The Vancouver Mandarin, with a management contract for the initial 25 years after opening in May 1984.

With the Company's hotels forming a group that extends from Hong Kong and Macau, and continues in Manila and then in Bangkok, Singapore, and Jakarta, the missing link — geographically — was Kuala Lumpur, capital of Malaysia. Early in 1983 the Company entered into an agreement with the owning company, Cosmopolitan Hotels (KL) Sdn. Bhd., and Mandarin International Hotels secured the management contract for The Oriental, Kuala Lumpur for 10 years after opening date due in 1986.

From what had been called by one commenta-tor 'a slow start,' it cannot be said that Hongkong Land and Mandarin International Hotels have been sluggish runners. Beginning in early 1974, with one deluxe hotel, The Mandarin, Hong Kong, a mere decade later MIHL now has nine hotels — five of them deluxe establishments and four in the first class category — with two more scheduled for completion soon. By mid-1986 the Company will have in its hotels 2,869 deluxe and 2,814 first class rooms and suites.

The far-reaching effects of The Mandarin in its first decade of existence are now clearly visible, and that first venture into the grand hotel business, which at the time was confidently described by some as 'Barton's folly,' has been vindicated in a very dramatic manner. Mandarin International Hotels has set the new standards both in deluxe and in first class accommodation for hotels in the East, and the fact that in some areas other companies have attempted to equal those standards is not only flattering but also proof of their viability.

New blood, new brief

Eric Waterhouse took over from Mullan Cunningham as managing director of Mandarin International Hotels Ltd. on October 15th, 1977.

'My brief was two-fold. The first was to put the hotels on to a more profitable footing. In 1978, Mandarin International Hotels made, after tax, HK$9.7 million profit. By 1983, the figure was HK$133 million. That gives an indication of the spread.

'We did not have very strong marketing then, and also had a couple of operations that were loss-making. The Convention Centre was losing money hand over fist, so one of the first things I had to do was to close it pretty rapidly — I was extremely unpopular for doing so because it was a place people liked to go to enjoy the pretty girls in the shows.

'Closing the Harbour Room in The Mandarin was another unpopular decision. It was rather hard, increasingly difficult in fact, to get the type of artists we wanted for the shows there, and prohibitively expensive.

'The second part of my brief was: to form a base for expansion, something which at that time had not been quantified at all.'

Eric Waterhouse is 'by nature, background, and training' a marketing man rather than an hotelier or a financier. It was, he thought, 'really a matter of examining *where* the Company's business came from.' A list of cities was drawn up where it was thought Mandarin International Hotels should have a presence.

Eric Waterhouse went on to look in detail at each hotel operation in turn with a view to improving them in various ways, not least in their physical aspect. That is not always an easy thing to do. And he echoes Peter Stafford's maxim in relation to proposed alterations to The Mandarin's public rooms: 'Anything that has become an institution needs courage to change.'

Definition for a Mandarin

'The basic philosophy that was beginning to emerge went something like this: a Mandarin hotel should be sited in a city centre, should be *grande luxe*, and must have a strong attraction for its *local* market as well as for visitors.'

Developing the strength of general managers was another goal — encouraging them to be at one and the same time profit-oriented and also the *patrons* in the traditional meaning of that word, the meeters and greeters. As the hotel business becomes more and more competitive, the need to find just the right men for this becomes ever more important.

Factors in expansion

In the past ten years Mandarin International Hotels has expanded phenomenally, but rationally. As Eric Waterhouse sees this, there are two factors underlying the process. First: 'If the location is not right, don't go in.' And second: 'There is the vital factor of getting the right partners, people with the same ambition as our own — that is, modestly, to have the best hotel in each city in which we operate. Partners must also be prepared to look at hotels as a long-term investment and therefore be financially strong.

'Apart from Tokyo, where one day we would like to be, Mandarin International Hotels is in almost every key city in the Far East. It was obvious that the next region we should consider would be the far side of the Pacific rim. Vancouver is really a test case for the Company's expansion into North America. We have there a very good site, and a very supportive local partner. A favourable factor in selecting Vancouver is that the city has a large Chinese population and its business connections with Hong Kong are considerable and growing.

'One thing for sure is that we are confident in Mandarin's future but like all companies we need to consolidate from time to time — then we can expand again slowly but surely — we have never had ambitions to be the biggest hotel group, only the best.'

The Mandarin International Magazine

From the start, The Mandarin published its own house magazine for the entertainment of its guests. In the first few years The Mandarin appeared irregularly and dealt mostly with Hong Kong — more especially with tourist Hong Kong. In those days there was comparatively little information available for tourists and other guests about the city and its amenities, other than that in the Tourist Association brochures. And Hong Kong was not then quite the well known destinaion that it now is. Tourism was still little developed and the flood-gates of Hong Kong's industry and international banking were yet to open, bringing with them a great surge of visitors.

As those aspects of Hong Kong developed, the magazine gradually became more sophisticated, tackling more interesting topics, and illustrating them with better photographs.

The editorship was taken by Kai-yin Lo, the dynamic public relations manager of The Mandarin, in late 1967, and under her direction found new subjects and treated them in a lively manner.

By 1974 Linda McCall had become editor and the articles began to carry bylines of such renowned correspondents as Dennis Bloodworth, the late Richard Hughes, Anthony Lawrence, Robert Shaplen of The New Yorker, and others.

By the time the present writer became editor in 1976 there were several hotels in The Mandarin International Hotels' group, and it became logical to rename the magazine **The Mandarin International**, and to run stories on the countries in which they are situated, as well as on the amenities of those new hotels. This approach, together with a process of redesigning the layout and updating of the style of the magazine has continued down to the present, when there are three issues per annum.

The magazine has introduced each new hotel as it was built and opened, giving some idea of its facilities, furnishing, and setting, and attempting to add articles on the people and places within reach of the guests. By now there are more hotels in the group than there is room in the magazine for stories on each region, and it is not possible to enlarge the magazine to accommodate more pages. The rich diversity of the lands and peoples of Southeast Asia, one of the world's most fascinating regions, provides, however, an infinity of material for the photographers and writers whose contributions reflect the region for The Mandarin's guests.

Copies of **The Mandarin International** go regularly to selected former guests of The Mandarin, as well as being placed in suites and rooms of all the Company's hotels

The Mandarin's Rolls Royce and Mercedes fleet with chauffeurs and chef concierge Giovanni Valenti. The chef concièrge heads a small department which is one of the busiest and most important in the hotel. His very visible presence in the lobby makes him the man everyone asks for help — a picnic on a junk, a reservation on Concorde from New York next Wednesday, can you wrap and freight this antique I just purchased? And a hundred other requests. It is his porters who make the baggage appear in your room almost at the same time as you are escorted to it — and never a suitcase to be seen in the lobby. Speaking a number of languages, he is everybody's helpful friend, an essential link between guests and management, and between guests and the world of Hong Kong

Re-emphasising the Priorities — Hofer and French

When Andreas Hofer was appointed general manager of The Mandarin on the first of November 1975, he was probably the youngest, most all-round qualified, and experienced hotelier of that time.

What was it like to take over The Mandarin at that moment — to take over an hotel which had suffered a dramatic drop in its occupancy rates in 1974 and 1975 in the wake of the oil crisis; an hotel which, moreover, was facing large competition in the shape of numbers of new hotels coming on stream — The Lee Gardens, The Excelsior, The Plaza in Causeway Bay, The Furama in central Hong Kong; and in Tsimshatsui, The Sheraton and Holiday Inn? And world recession did not look like just quietly or even soon going away.

How did Hofer tackle this tricky, even threatening situation?

New approach

'I couldn't possibly just let the hotel run on in the same way. That much was obvious. I had to do something quick and drastic, otherwise I wouldn't be proving myself worthy of the job. What I did was to take an in-depth look at the entire sales and marketing operation. Of course the result was that a few heads rolled, and I was sorry about that. But it couldn't be helped. In many ways I was lucky in that I had had plenty of opportunity in the past to draw on the large experience of Tony Ross and Peter Stafford. That helped me a lot. I was able to pick out their strong points and disregard other elements.

'What it amounted to — to sum up what I did — was to introduce a more streamlined type of management. I didn't want to run The Mandarin entirely by myself. I introduced a

controlled system of delegation to the heads of departments, and let them get on with their business in a controlled manner.'

Delegation and control there had of course always been in varying degrees under the previous two general managers. But under Andy Hofer the process was given more definitive form and carried out more closely and methodically.

Reacting to Peter Stafford's words about having to be possessive about the hotel, Hofer countered: 'Yes, certainly, you have to be possessive about your hotel. But my thoughts on managing go also in another direction. Now — nine years after the time I took over — I'm sure that no one can manage an hotel with 600 rooms and 3,000 people passing through its restaurants daily, all by himself. So, highly controlled delegation of responsibility is absolutely essential these days. I started by introducing a programme of daily routine meetings with heads of all departments, and also — this is highly important — timing them so that people didn't spend their whole day locked up round the meeting table.'

Difficult task

To follow in the footsteps of a vibrant, versatile, very visible personality such as Peter Stafford, cannot have been easy. Hofer's approach to the job was a different one altogether. 'There are 1,200 employees in The Mandarin. It simply isn't possible to be on friendly terms with all of them. There isn't *time* for that, just as there isn't *time* for being totally visible to the hundreds of hotel guests — and at the same time imagine that you are really managing an hotel.

Andreas Hofer

Coming originally to The Mandarin in 1966, Andreas Hofer — Andy as everyone calls him — took the job of restaurant manager of the Grill early in that year under the management of Tony Ross. In a few months he was promoted to restaurant and banquet manager, a position he held for a couple of years until 1968.

'At that time,' he says, looking back, 'I was a relatively young man, and I was happy with the position.' The following year brought promotion again, to food and beverage manager, and he kept that job for what he calls 'a rather long period of five years. By that time I was beginning to feel a bit restless, so I approached the Company. I was looking for something more responsible. What was in my mind was the formation of Mandarin International Hotels in 1974, with the opportunities that it seemed to offer.'

The Company offered a senior management training programme, what he calls 'investing a bit of money in my further education.' Continuing his education the Company sent him to Cornell University to brush up on financial aspects, and then to the Fairmont Hotel, San Francisco for four months in several of its areas, and he was then promised he would be taking over one of the Company's new hotels as general manager. By this time he had been away from his family for well over six months, and just as he was about to return to Hong Kong he was asked to go to Las Vegas to study convention and entertainment activity — the aim being that he should return as project manager of the new Convention Centre being built in Hong Kong.

This he did, returning to Hong Kong late in 1974. Having successfully opened the Convention Centre in September 1975, he began to hear rumours of Peter Stafford's impending departure from The Mandarin, and on enquiring from the Company was told that in fact he was to take over The Mandarin as general manager in November 1975

Hofer infers that nowadays the time has gone when such a style of management in a large, complex hotel is consistent with profitability. 'To make the transition from the one style to the other was a tough task. For a time I had to perpetuate the PR style of management to some extent, while instituting my new system and style. This meant at first that I was putting in much more time than most hotel managers. But this was a necessary bridge from one style and method to the other. In the end I think it succeeded tolerably well.

Delegation

'One of the keys is to delegate much to the resident manager — at first I had Peter French and then later Wolfgang Hultner. But I don't forget that I also had luck on my side. Not all at first, but certainly in the boom years of 1978 to 1981.

'I was very young, only 36, when I took over The Mandarin. That, in the mid-seventies, for an internationally known five-star hotel, was a bit risky. I was conscious that I was being observed from all quarters — by other hoteliers, and by the Company too. It made me all the more determined to make a good job of it. Despite the work-load initially, it seemed to me to be necessary to enter into whatever outside activities in the Hong Kong community I could. I was offered the vice-chairmanship of the Hong Kong Hotels Association, a position I occupied for several years, becoming chairman in 1979 — a great honour. The government appointed me as one of two men heading the Hong Kong Hotels Catering and Travel Board.' Such activities, he felt were good value for The Mandarin.

In common with other hotels, The Mandarin went — and still goes — through various phases in its operations. The Imperial Banquet that Peter Stafford masterminded was a huge success in promoting not only its culinary capabilities but also the international character of the hotel. There followed an era when the Harbour Room restaurant was completely redesigned once more, by Don Ashton, to accommodate the then current practice of adding cabaret to dining. Later still came the phase when supper theatre came into vogue and the restaurant saw such review-type entertainments as *The 20s and All that Jazz, Oh! Coward* and others in the years 1977 and 1978.

The fifteenth anniversary of The Mandarin's opening was celebrated in glittering fashion by inviting a large number of distinguished guests to an evening dress reception at which the Hong Kong Philharmonic Orchestra played, and a fifteen-storey birthday cake stood amid the elegant scene in the lobby.

End of an era

At fifteen, an hotel needs upgrading and modification. Numbers of such schemes had of course been carried out under Tony Ross and Peter Stafford, but in the lean years perhaps less was done than could have been to maintain the highest standards. 'Anything major that you do in an hotel,' says Andy Hofer, 'needs an immense amount of detailed planning to be a success — and, equally, so as to interfere as little as possible with the normal running of the hotel and the comfort of the guests. The era of cabaret ended, largely because the artists priced themselves out of that particular market, which is the size of

Last of the Harbour Room

The last night at the Harbour Room restaurant was for many a moment of regret and nostalgia. The souvenir menu was prefaced by a brief history.

'In September 1963, the forerunner of the Harbour Room, The Button Supper Club, opened on the Roof Garden floor of The Mandarin.

'It proved so popular during the cabaret boom of the 60's that even when the top floor was reorganised and the swimming pool closed, it was decided that The Mandarin still needed a sophisticated international çabaret venue.

'So it was that in 1968, the curtain went up on the Kessler Twins, and the Harbour Room opened.

'Over the past 11 years a host of international artistes have starred here. Dave Allen, Les Dawson, and Bob Monkhouse have made the Harbour Room rock with laughter. Eartha Kitt, Matt Monro and Billy Daniels have filled the room with their special songs, while the ever popular Seekers and Sandpipers made the Harbour Room their Hong Kong base.

'Robert Morley and Barry Humphries defy any kind of classification!

'From comedians, singers, and groups the Harbour Room launched into musical revue and in April 1978, "Oh! Coward" opened with leading West End stars David Kernan, John Moffatt, and June Ritchie. This was followed later by "The 20's and All That Jazz." Both were smash hits.

'But times change and all good things must end. So after 11 years we bid farewell to the Harbour Room and we now look forward with great excitement to October when, in its place, The Mandarin will be opening a fine, exclusive French restaurant "Pierrot."

'The decor of Pierrot has been designed by the leading international design consultant Don Ashton whose work already graces The Mandarin hotels throughout the region. The restaurant will be elegant and intimate, seating just 75 guests.

'To complement Pierrot, the Lookout Lounge is being completely redesigned and will be called the Harlequin Bar.'

a restaurant typified by the Harbour Room. They became too expensive for the operation to make financial success. And another problem was how, in Hong Kong, to book artists 'back to back' — one show finishing and the next opening the following day. It was harder here than in Europe and America.'

Pierrot

Another aspect that conditioned the first phase of extensive changes was that The Mandarin had always wanted to have a top class speciality restaurant. So, after thirteen years (and 'sadly' as Andy Hofer comments), the Harbour Room, successor to The Button of early days, was removed. In its place was built Pierrot, the superbly designed restaurant specialising in French cuisine, a small — only 75-seat — luxuriously comfortable environment for the enjoyment of some of Hong Kong's finest food. With it came a new lounge bar, The Harlequin, in a complementary style. And, in the remaining area, for Pierrot is much smaller than the Harbour Room was, an indoor pool in Roman style with adjoining health club were constructed. The elegance of the pool is unique in Hong Kong, cool, pillared, classically restrained.

Phase two of The Mandarin's renewal programme was also initiated by Andy Hofer, although he was not there in his capacity as general manager to see it finished. Among important aspects were the complete renewal of the telephone system by the installation of an electronic facility which takes up less than half the space of the old one and is ultra-efficient and flexible in its multiple functions.

This was followed by the relocation of the Coffee Shop. The original Causette was never, perhaps, anyone's favourite place. It was too small and somehow rather dark — not in fact, but in the impression it gave. The decision to construct a new, much roomier, and up-to-date coffee shop, entailed, however, a whole complicated series of terminations of leases and renewal of other leases for short periods of shops located on the proposed site at the diagonally opposite corner of the ground floor to the Causette. The problem was to get all the leases to terminate at the same time, and to avoid having any shop left vacant until the lease on the last shop terminated. Such an exercise, requiring tact with shop-owners who have been good tenants for many a year, is rather easier described than accomplished.

But accomplished it was. The Causette, probably not much regretted, was replaced by the new Coffee Shop, called just that, designed with a combination of elegance and functionalism. Its popularity was immediate and has remained very great — lunchtime every weekday sees a line of hungry and determined persons waiting outside in the rear arcade of the hotel for their turn to eat there.

Business centre

Hand in hand with the relocation of the coffee shop went the enlargement of the lobby area to take in that of the Causette, thus accommodating a business centre — another amenity not in the hotel book anywhere in the world when The Mandarin was built. This extension of the public space is a cool place, all black marble and gold, comfortable, and providing an efficient and much used service to guests. The argument that most businessmen staying at The Mandarin

The new Coffee Shop

have secretarial and other facilities in large offices of their own or affiliated companies in Hong Kong, proved to be only partly valid. The use made of the business centre proves the point.

'I had gone,' says Andy Hofer a little ruefully, 'by the time those changes were complete.'

'Like every hotelier in a great hotel, you have your great days and others when things go against you. My memories of my long stay with The Mandarin are mostly of hard work, but with its rewards. When the world stays with you and you are host to its crowned heads, its most powerful politicians, the heads of its largest business empires, life smiles on you and your hotel. When His Excellency the governor takes the trouble to congratulate you on some official function well carried through, that makes it all worthwhile. And,

aside from such highlights, there is a continuing reward in seeing the satisfaction of the guests as a whole.'

New general manager

Andreas Hofer left The Mandarin at the end of 1981 to take up the position of Regional Director of Operations in Mandarin International Hotels Limited.

His successor as general manager at The Mandarin was Peter French who had, in Hofer's time, been resident manager in the hotel. From that position he had moved to The Excelsior in 1975 as resident manager, and assumed the general managership of the hotel in 1978. On the first of January, 1982 he moved to the general manager's seat in The Mandarin, no stranger to the details of its operation.

Peter J. French

Peter French was born in England in 1949 and graduated from Birmingham University, subsequently being awarded a Fellowship of the Hotel Catering and Institutional Management Association. His career began as hotel officer aboard the Cunard Line's Queen Elizabeth and Queen Elizabeth 2, during which he spent training time in hotels around the world — the Piccadilly and the Mayfair in London, the Plaza in New York, and the Fontainbleau in Miami. In 1971 he moved to the hotels division of Cunard before joining the Cunard Convention Centre as food and beverage manager.

On his arrival in Hong Kong, Peter French took up the position of resident manager of the Company's flagship hotel, The Mandarin, and three years later went over to The Mandarin's sister hotel, The Excelsior. After four years there, during which The Excelsior was included as an HRI hotel, he rejoined The Mandarin at the age of thirty-three as Hong Kong's youngest general manager, in January, 1982.

In that same year The Mandarin achieved the eminence of the world's number two hotel — with The Oriental in Bangkok taking the number one spot in an opinion poll conducted by the influential financial journal The Institutional Investor.

Now, during The Mandarin's coming-of-age celebrations, Peter French continues an ongoing programme of upgrading and modernization of his now internationally famous hotel

'An average day starts at 8:00 a.m. I come down to the duty manager's office and have a meeting with the on-coming duty manager and the night manager. We run through the night manager's report book (a log of comments and observations on everything of note that occurred between midnight and eight in the morning). These books are highly interesting, recording as they do not only what happened, but such things as early arrivals of guests, the incidents during the previous night, any sort of trouble whatsoever. Then we run through last night's occupancy to see if anything special needs to be done in regard to that.'

Morning walk

Peter French is a tall man, a big man with a ready smile that gives an impression of friendly mildness. A rather quiet voice in meetings can turn incisive without getting any louder — and you know then how firmly he is in charge.

Next on his agenda is to have a walk around the hotel, visiting all areas where breakfast is being served, seeing room service, banqueting, all the restaurants, and the ground floor by now well into its stride in the new day.

'Then I take a walk *outside* the hotel, checking everything from the flowers and planting, the flags fluttering above the main entry, to the condition of the building's exterior. After that I pick a cross-section of rooms and make spot checks on their condition, and on that of rooms prepared for special guests. Then comes 'back of the house' — laundry, kitchens, and up to the pool area, generally being cleaned at this time, and up to the roof. This often takes me to 8:30 or 8:45.'

Certainly before 9 a.m. he is in his office. 'The daily business is all trace-filed so that anything pertinent to that day will come up. I prepare for my first meeting which is with the front of house people at 9:15. Really my office ought to be on the ground floor instead of the second — I spend a lot of time running up and down stairs. There isn't time to wait for the lift!'

Guests come first

At the meeting are: the resident manager, director of sales, public relations manager, front office manager, concierge, and telephone manager. Peter French runs through the list of guests expected during the day, noting any special requests or other matters that are out of the usual routine.

And VIP arrivals are dealt with. A journalist from San Francisco is staying at The Peninsula and wants to come to The Mandarin also, but this is a matter of juggling dates with him since the hotel is full. Then there is a problem of squeezing in some important executive of Jardine, Matheson and Company; and what sort of gift from the management to put in the room of the vice-mayor of Shanghai when he arrives with his party. The shortage of rooms is acute and several guests who may want to extend their stay will really have to go at the times they originally stated. Regrets, but other guests are booked.

The meeting proceeds swiftly, quietly, all participants ready with answers, taking notes. The impression of an efficient front of house team is inescapable, ready to make decisions on their own within the framework, to give detailed attention to the requirements of all guests.

Gems from the Night Manager's Report Book

From midnight until 8 a.m. the overall control of the running of The Mandarin is in the hands of the night manager.

He keeps a log that records details of such expectable events as how many people checked in or out of the hotel, the time of arrival of the two morning newspapers, irregularities such as finding unlocked a door that ought to be locked, the progress of whatever repairs or small repainting jobs, or shampooing of furniture, that may be in progress during those night hours.

Other comments are on matters slightly more irregular. A judicious selection from the past year or so includes the following:

'16 November. 04.10. Mr. F.W. (room number supplied) phoned up the assistant manager's office, the enquiry desk, and room service asking if we could arrange for him some 'fun' or 'entertainment.' All respondents told him No, and Sorry.'

Forty minutes later, a further entry recounts: 'Room service captain reported a nude man was seen strolling in the corridor (near Mr. F.W.'s room) holding a bottle of wine. (Night manager) went straight up with security but could find no one there. Believe Mr. F.W. hid back in his room after knowing being seen.'

It was an amusing night, if perhaps a trifle tiresome from the staff's point of view, a few days later.

'25 November. 06:00. A European lady came into the hotel and slept on one of the chairs in the foyer. Tried to wake her up but she went back to her dream soon after . . . . Security was informed and woke her up again. But she claimed that the hotel foyer is open to everyone. After we explained to her that we can't accept people sleeping in the lobby, she left in five minutes.'

Some mornings later: '06:15. Twenty-five well dressed people came in with several bottles of champagne (almost finished) and wanted breakfast. All were directed to take a seat in the lobby until the Coffee Shop opens. No inconvenience caused to hotel guests during the breakfast service.'

Another night, great discretion was used in peculiar circumstances: '01:30. Room service was told not to send boiled eggs to room 920 in the morning as, upon doing a checking tour of the 9th floor, Raymond Chan (night manager) happened to see a Mr. F. from room 922 laughing and writing something on the breakfast ring (hung on door handle) of room 920 — see attached copy. The night manager then approached him and explained nicely that by doing this the hotel will be in trouble in the morning. But Mr. F. said: "Don't worry, he's my friend, he did this to me one time before. So I'm doing it to him — I just want to give him two more boiled eggs!" He then went back to his room.'

Another early morning in the same month the log reports:

'1:30 am. Received a call from (a bar in the neighbourhood of the hotel) that they will

close soon, and could we sent a car to escort Mr. T.J. of room 1810 back to the hotel. A porter went in a taxi but Mr. T.J. asked him to leave, saying he can manage by himself. He returned at 1:50 am. and continued his dream in the Captain's Bar.' The night manager's delicate use of the word 'dream' is noteworthy!

Guests frequently discover at unlikely hours that they lack some essential item of toiletry. One case is typical of many:

'05:35 Room 1620. Mr. E.J. called reception requesting shaving cream and aftershave lotion, and could he buy them from the Health Centre now. Explained that the Health Centre doesn't open till 07:00 but we can send him some shaving cream. Asistant housekeeper advised to do so, and later advised he could't find any shaving cream but had sent up a battery shaver! I then lent my own Aramis 900 and shaving cream, which made the guest's wife remark. "I must say The Mandarin is the best of hotels!" Shouldn't these courtesy facilities' adds the night manager, 'always be available in the housekeeping office?'

'02:45. "EAT MHDARIN IGSILLR Closed At Present" was found displayed on the first floor Mandarin Grill closure sign. It should read "The Mandarin grill is closed at present." Now rectified.'

Surprising things happen occasionally. '07:10 to 07:35. Noticed twenty school children waiting in the lobby. They were to be picked up for a Macau tour. No action was taken as they were behaving themselves, but I told the night concierge to advise the Macau Able Tour Company to arrange a proper place in future.'

One entry records the case of the unfortunate night manager who, in thwarting a drunk and rather well known lady of the town from mounting to a guest's room from the lobby, was attacked by her with the stiletto heel of her shoe, followed by threats that "her boyfriends will be waiting for me" in the morning when I leave.'

Finally there is the story of the guest who, near to his departure, discovered that he was missing his pyjamas. They were, happily, discovered by calling the laundry which washes the sheets, having been inadvertently rolled up in them and sent there by mistake. The laundry rushed the missing item to the hotel in time for the guest's departure.

There is, now and then in the reports, a straightforward note on the arrival at 02:00 or some time in that region of a gentleman resident on one of the islands near to Hong Kong who, having long since missed the last ferry home, arrives luggage-less and badly in need of a comfortable night's lodging — and who is invariably accommodated.

The flexibility of The Mandarin's service is of a kind to remind one of those marvellous hotels in Europe in the earlier part of this century whose amenities were such that the most exacting guests, at the most improbable hours, had merely to ask for the most improbable things, to have their desires added unto them with a smile

The Connaught Rooms prepared for a cocktail reception

Arrangements for a function hosted by a large international bank are run through, and those for a cocktail party to be held by The Hongkong Land Company, the lobby staff to be alerted for the arrival of the managing director.

Essential details

More 'domestic' details come up. A new employee has just been taken on, starting in a couple of months' time. She is being married before then. Mr. French reminds the relevant person to send her a congratulatory message.

The reprinting of tariff forms is discussed, and new menus for the Grill — the present ones will last for some months more but the new year must be marked by design changes. 'Who put down that piece of carpeting in the shopping arcade on the ground floor?' asks Peter French. The resident manager replies: 'It was put there when there was a water leak in the typhoon, so as to prevent dirt being carried into the lobby. It ought to have been taken away by now.'

'Yes, it ought to have been,' replies Peter French dryly.

Then: 'We have a telex from Mr. Brown requesting room 2112 or 2012 as usual, otherwise he won't come.' Amused smiles all round. This has obviously happened many times before. Part of the function of a good hotel is to humour the small and the larger whims of its guests.

And so the meeting continues, briskly, low-key, breaking up immediately business is finished. There is about fifteen minutes gap in

For a major dinner party the Connaught Rooms provide an elegant, luxurious setting

which the general manager returns to his desk for paperwork in preparation for his next meeting at 10 a.m.

Promptly at that time the resident manager, executive housekeeper, chief engineer, and (if it is a Tuesday) the health centre supervisor, take their places, discussing a point or two among themselves until Peter French appears.

Chandeliers and shoes

Reports that the huge Venetian chandeliers in the lobby have been cleaned, and that errant carpet at the back door arcade has in fact now gone, are heard. Problems with double glazing are gone into, as are some slight difficulties with detailing in the newly redesigned Grill — these to be brought up with Don Ashton, the designer, in the afternoon.

Since the Grill was re-made, taking in part of the ladies room on the same floor, there have been complaints that there is no longer a full-length mirror there. This has to be further discussed. The chief engineer reports he has adjusted the level of the airconditioning in relation to the prevailing outside temperature. The dates for spring cleaning of the 22nd floor are finalised and it is confirmed that all departments who will be involved — from the front desk to the floor staff and various contractors — have been notified and have agreed to the dates.

'Why was the time clock at the employees's entrance unplugged yesterday?' asks Peter French. The chief engineer says it cannot be unplugged because it is *wired* in, but that somehow the power cord became disconnect-

Everything ready for a private Chinese dinner party in the Kublai Khan room

ed. This has now been rectified in such a way that it cannot happen again. Someone else remarks that in any case the time at which an employee arrives for duty can be double-checked as the names and times are entered when uniforms are collected.

'What happened with the complaint from Mr. Smith about his missing light brown shoes?' The housekeeper reports the room boys say this guest had a large number of shoes which he sent to be polished, and that there was no light brown pair among them. It is decided this is a case for tactful words with the guest.

'I gather,' remarks Peter French with a wry smile, 'we have another of those freak phone bills — this one for a seven-hour overseas call costing $4,000!' General laughter. Everyone knows that sometimes when the guest or his overseas correspondent fails to hang up pro-

perly, this can happen. The telephone manager will take the usual action to which the telephone company usually responds by cancelling the charges. Peter French jokes: 'The last chap whom this happened to, said to me he hadn't talked to his wife that long in all their married life. But that was the fourteen-hour call!'

Thus the second meeting of the morning ends. It is now just after 10:30 a.m. Time for the general manager to collect his thoughts in preparation for the food and beverage meeting at 11 a.m.

Chefs talking

At that time the conference room is visually enlivened. Among the uniform black jackets and pinstriped trousers of most participants, the executive chef enters in crisp white uniform and wearing his tall, equally

Dinner for four in the Grill

crisp white cap. With him come the food and beverage manager and his assistant, together with the banquet manager.

The meeting begins with a recap of what was said at an earlier one on the subject of the new menus for the Grill. Some increase in food prices indicates the need to alter prices of certain dishes. Points in advertising strategy for the restaurants are discussed. And the general manager asks for a sales analysis on afternoon teas in the Clipper Lounge where the variety of cakes and sandwiches served as an item involves several different varieties of both. It is important to discover the precise item which is not so popular, and to delete it.

The foreign bank's reception of this evening is discussed in its food and beverage connotations, and also the reception for Hong-kong Land. The number of supervisors and waiters required is decided, and details of the equipment required and the floral decorations is stated by the food and beverage manager.

A comparison of meat prices from various sources is decided upon. 'How do the red currants on that sweet taste — not bitter, I hope?' says Peter French. 'And do you leave the stalk on or not?'

A variation in the type of bread for a certain layered sandwich is discussed after Peter French — just returned from London — remarks that it seemed popular in certain hotels there. New fish tanks appear to be necessary in the kitchen of the Man Wah restaurant.

Staff training

Discussion turns on exchange of chefs with various hotels for training purposes, and the merits and demerits are thrashed out. 'We don't want to go into the training centre business for the world,' says Peter French.

The Smoking Grotto

One evening when Andy Hofer was dining with some guests at the top of the hotel, a page boy hurried in to give him a note. The note contained the message that smoke was pouring from the Grotto. Hastily excusing himself on the plea of an urgent overseas call, he rushed to the lift. 'Exactly what one should not do in a fire, as we all know, is to take the lift!' he says, mocking himself.

Now, the Grotto is the unofficial but universally used name of what lies behind the onyx wall with the Chinese gilded carvings in the lounge area of the main lobby. Many guests have seen cleaning amahs in their immaculate white shirts with black trousers (literally in the Cantonese, sam fu, shirt and trousers) push that wall at a certain point, and the wall yields, opening on to a dark interior space. In the space, which in fact lies behind the message and information desk, behind the key boxes, various cleaning materials, old files, and other sundry items that have no more convenient place are kept.

'Some naughty office boy had been in there for an illicit cigarette, and had either left it burning or not properly stubbed it out. When I got down, the lobby was full of smoke which at first had been seen oozing from under the Grotto door. Then someone decided to investigate, opened the door, thus adding the necessary oxygen, and great clouds of thick smoke belched forth. The fire brigade was already on its way, and since there was no apparent flame, and none of us could enter the Grotto without asphixiation, we waited for them.' Andy Hofer tells the story very amusingly. 'When the first fireman, wearing breathing apparatus, went in, he almost at once emerged bearing an armful of smouldering old files. And that was that.' It is not hard to imagine the next morning's meeting with the department heads concerned.

The Grotto is still there, a source of momentary wonderment to guests as that elegant wall gives to the touch where no discontinuity in its surface is noticeable. 'It's really where the telephone exchange ought to be, but even with the new and compact system, there isn't enough room inside.'

'That's the point.' He calls for revenue figures from a certain recent banquet, and the meeting ends with discussions on total budgets for the food and beverage department as a whole.

Because the day is Tuesday, a personnel and training meeting is scheduled to follow immediately on the food and beverage one, and the all-male cast round the table changes to a female one — the personnel manager and training manager.

'How is the planning for the staff Christmas party getting along,' asks Peter French. A brief discussion follows on the arrangements being made.

Problems relating to trainees of certain categories are aired. 'Don't be surprised when you find a request for the purchase of children's books on your desk,' remarks the training manager. 'We are finding that in many ways they are better for starting some trainees off, than the textbooks we are using. Especially with those who have almost no English at the beginning.'

A new telephone operator has finished her training. Two apprentices from The Mandarin have made it in the competition for the top ten in Hong Kong hotels.

It appears that recently in various Hong Kong hotels there has been a series of thefts from rooms by people posing as employees. This is a problem in any hotel with large numbers of staff who don't all know each other. It is decided to put notices in the staff areas urging anyone with any suspicions to contact the personnel manager immediately. The matter will be mentioned in the next staff magazine, and some posters will also be put up.

With such topics as these, discussed in an informal way with no wastage of words, but time for a joke or two, this last of the morning's meetings breaks up.

Routine

It is now about midday. 'I have one extra meeting every morning, such as the personnel and training one,' say Peter French. 'Monday sees me at 11:00 in head office where I report on the weekly working of the hotel, and on the figures. To be a general manager today you have to be a businessman. You have to show the best financial return, to achieve the budget. At the end of the day that's your number one priority. It is different from former times, or rather perhaps I should say that it is the same but that the *emphasis* is a little different. My main objective has to be to achieve the financial target.'

Monday, head office; Tuesday, personnel and training; Wednesday, the executive committee meeting. 'This is a new thing. It's a discipline in which all sit down — the controller, resident manager, food and beverage manager, director of sales, public relations manager, personnel manager, and the executive housekeeper — and talk about things. *General* things. Such things as where we could improve. We look through questionnaires filled in by guests for some of these weak areas. We talk about strategy. It is all very casual in tone, but I think that if we didn't have this meeting we might not get round to thinking along those lines. It's something I introduced so that we all have time away from our particular work to talk — just to talk together.'

Thursday, advertising meeting; Friday, sales meeting. Friday afternoon, weekly finance meeting.

Then there are monthly meetings at various

The Mandarin's Distinguished Guests

Top: their Majesties the King and Queen of Tonga. Above: their Royal Highnesses Prince Bertil and Princess Lilian of Sweden with Sir Y.K. Kan. Above right: the President of India, His Excellency Giani Zail Singh, welcomed by the general manager, Peter French. Centre: Mr. René Lecler, author of The 300 Best Hotels in the World, *with Andreas Hofer (right) and his wife. Right: former United States President Gerald Ford and his wife*

Above left: Peter French welcomes His Serene Highness Prince Rainier III of Monaco and the late Princess Grace. Left: Miss Gina Lolobrigida in her suite. Top: former British Prime Minister Edward Heath welcomed by assistant manager Frederick Leung. Above: Robert Carrier, of restaurant and cookbook fame, tasting food by chefs from Hangchow in China who gave a four-week presentation of their food at the Man Wah restaurant

times in the afternoon. 'The heads of departments meeting on the first Wednesday of the month is basically me talking to the rest about how we've got on since last time. There are too many people present,' Peter French remarks, 'for this to be anything but a formal one. It's a sort of general knowledge meeting — so that, for example, there isn't a situation whereby someone in food and beverage is nearly totally ignorant of what is going on in the rest of the hotel.

'On the third Tuesday of each month there's the food and beverage control meeting in which we look at costs, at stores, at what to buy in terms of liquor and other things. We look at menus and attempt a menu analysis to see what items are going well. Nowadays, you see, the manager of the Man Wah restaurant — for instance — knows his budget for the year is just so much. And he's got to make it. If he's not looking like making it, he gets picked up at this meeting. This all sounds a bit like third degree, but it isn't. The idea is to give the man a goal. We didn't have this meeting before. And of course you obviously can't hold each man to his budget, but to talk about it and his performance gives him a reason other than the usual one of service. I believe in bringing people on, and this and other meetings are part of their general education.'

Last meetings

Three o'clock every third Thursday of the month brings the housekeeping meeting which 'has to do with costs and control of costs, and hence with profitability.' And it is followed by the engineering meeting. This, too, is a financial meeting dealing with heat, light, and power topics, with how much is spent on paint, varnish, oil, and so on.'

Turning to a chart on the wall of the conference room (where there are several others, including the meeting schedules) Peter French says: 'This one flabbergasted a group of visiting Chinese hoteliers!' The chart has no single heading but could in fact be called: *How to Run a Good Hotel.*

'That,' Peter French says, 'is my morning and some of my afternoon. By lunchtime I tour the restaurants, talk to people, spend time in the lobby downstairs. The wonderful thing about The Mandarin's lobby is that unlike that of most hotels everything that is going on is completely visible from one place or the other. This is useful. I can catch people I want to see as they come or go.'

Walkabout

His afternoons are mostly spent on administration and correspondence. 'At five-ish I walk through the Clipper Lounge which is usually full at that time, and then through the Harlequin Bar, and all the other outlets that are busy then. I spend more time in the lobby, check late arrivals, check V.I.P. rooms, and perhaps have a drink with some guests. I finish off at about 7 p.m. This is six days a week. The duty manager is responsible on Sundays, but I always do a general check.

'My biggest enemy is the clock. But fortunately I work well in stress situations. I would like to have more time to reflect. When I have to sign piles of cheques, thousands of them, it's so automatic that I actually do think then. There is always this question of how much time you can spend with the guests and how much time you *must* spend on the business and

When The Mandarin was built such things as Business Centres and Health Clubs were no part of the hotel scene. The elegant classical architecture of the pool in the Health Club now assorts well with the delicate elaboration of Chinese-style decor elsewhere in the hotel

administration side of being an hotelier. There is no easy answer.'

In fact each of the four general managers who have guided the fortunes of The Mandarin in its first 21 years has come up with a different answer, different at least in quantitative ways. Tony Ross, with the difficult task of opening a new hotel, was good at delegating, good at administration, and good with staff, but by nature not an easy mixer with all and sundry among the guests. Yet his was a successful term as general manager.

He was followed by an extremely social man, Peter Stafford, by nature a person whose prime interest is in other people, and in this respect an ideal general manager. During his term, he was easily the most visible of the four, tireless in moving round the hotel and seeing for himself, rather than delegating the various tasks to his subordinates, making the attempt to know each member of the staff. The fact that The Mandarin is a focus of social life in the particular way it is in Hong Kong, was probably initially Peter Stafford's doing. It has to be remembered that in his time, for any hotel in Hong Kong the competition was not nearly as severe as it is today. The priorities for a general manager could be different in their emphasis, as Peter French says.

Stafford was followed by Andreas Hofer who began the process of shifting and re-emphasising those priorities, and carried it through vigorously and to great effect in very difficult times. Along with his predecessors, Hofer made many changes in the fabric of the hotel, and planned yet others which came to fruition after he moved on. Under Peter French still further changes in the hotel have been made, and doubtless will be made. A public place requires renewal, upgrading from time to time in part due to wear and tear, but also, importantly, because of changes in public taste. Just as business centres were not a requirement in the hotels of two decades ago, the decor of, say, the Clipper Lounge and the Grill was fashionable when it was first done, but looked less good when the time came to redesign it.

The Grill was completely redesigned by Don Ashton in a brilliantly flexible and luxurious manner. The setting gives each table a hint of privacy without any feeling of isolation. Lighting is carefully soft and flattering. What always was the most popular restaurant in Central for lunch still is, and the new décor encourages dining in its inimitable relaxed atmosphere.

The numerous alterations to the top floor reflect the same necessity to acknowledge changing public taste as the years go by. 'The Mandarin' as Peter Stafford has said, 'has probably made more money than most other hotels of its size. But to do so it has had to spend a lot.'

The process must necessarily be ongoing, something that bodes well for the hotel and its guests in the future.

Embedded in Central Hong Kong, The
Mandarin seen from the busy harbour

Morning, Noon, and Night

A significant part of the pleasure of staying in a fine hotel is that everything works, and works with apparently effortless ease. The secret of running a fine hotel is to keep it that way. The guests are always the number one consideration. They have absolute priority; and, as Peter Stafford says, with good manners, in the widest sense of the phrase, and the minimum of fuss, the guests' stay in the hotel comes to resemble travelling in a Rolls Royce — maximum comfort, a smooth ride, everything to hand that can reasonably, even sometimes unreasonably, be expected.

Implicit in this state of affairs is the removal of the cares and the chores of daily routine. Whether the guest is on business or pleasure the functions of the hotel must include the *aura* of welcome along with the words. This means many things, but it certainly means willing and intelligent service by the staff at all levels, at all times, from general manager to doorman, from roomboy to telephonist.

Changing needs

All guests have differing needs, put different emphasis on this or that requirement. Some are more personal — the loan of a hairdryer, the stitching on of a button — but all have to be envisaged. For this and for other reasons the quality of service has to be unfailingly excellent. So has the quality of the food in the restaurants or from room service. There have to be facilities for quiet talks between friends or business associates to take place at ease and in the kind of comfort that is part of such occasions.

Apart from the normal services of the hotel there is a constant need by both business people and travellers for assistance of all kinds on local matters — about how long it might take to reach a place where an appointment has been made, about where would be the best shop to buy Chinese silk or ivory carvings, and often much more outlandish things. The Mandarin is used to such questions as one from an American couple who, prior to their arrival, telexed with the request that a Chinese fortune teller be found for them. One was found and the details telexed back within an hour or two.

New amenities

Recent years have brought changes in the spread of guest requirements. Business centres and health clubs that were not thought of in days gone by have become an essential part of the hotel's services. Such facilities as international direct dialling by the guests have come into use recently, as have closed circuit TV and other less obvious things.

All those aspects of the hotel and its services contribute to the feeling of relaxation, of having the time and the right place to be at ease after a taxing day or even just a round of shopping and sightseeing. The guest returns to the hotel with the knowledge that he or she will find the kind of comfort and food and drink that restore the flagging spirit. Not only that, but something much less easy to define — an atmosphere that is in all ways congenial. However fine the linen sheets, however elegant the decor in public and private spaces, however well equipped the bathrooms, it is the quality of the human services that in the end produce the guest's feeling of physical comfort and induce in him the sense of a welcoming friendliness; and keep doing that.

The only people who ever sleep in The

1974

1984

The Cheung Family at The Mandarin

A long time ago a carpenter called Cheung Wah came to Hong Kong from his native Canton. He joined the Gloucester Hotel in that capacity, and as his sons grew to man's estate, one by one they too joined the hotel. With his eldest son Kwok Wing, he came over to The Mandarin when it opened. Soon the younger brothers joined the hotel staff — Kwok Hung, then Kwok Kuen, Kwok Fai, and lastly, in 1971, the 21-year-old Kwok Kee.

The father Kwok Wah has now passed away and the eldest son, Kwok Wing, is no longer with the hotel, but the four remaining brothers are still all employed in various positions in the engineering department

Veteran Staff

About 140 of the staff of The Mandarin either came over for the opening from the old Gloucester Hotel or joined in the first year of business. Here they are — the assistant manager of the Grill, the chefs, barmen, waiters, engineers, roomboys, amahs, and all the others — happy to be part of The Mandarin, proud to have played their part in making it what it is today

In 1981 The Mandarin team came first in the inter-hotel soccer matches. Back row, left to right: Lau Yiu Wo, Lee Kar Chun, Lam Shiu Cheong, Joseph Chan, Wong Sing Yuen, Andy Yip, Yip Kam Cheung, Danny Wong. Front row, left to right: Cheung Kwok Kuen, Chan Yiu Fai, Tony Tang, Mah Wai Tong, Lau Chin Pang, Johnson Tse

Mandarin in Hong Kong, or in any of the Company's other hotels (apart from a clutch of general and resident managers in each one) — are the guests. Morning, noon, and night everyone else in the hotel is hard at work.

Most of these people are never seen by guests who in fact see very little of the staff apart from those behind the front desk, and in the bars and restaurants. Besides those, guests probably encounter a few room-service personnel, perhaps one of the housekeepers doing her rounds, and possibly the roomboy who comes to turn down the beds, a messenger or two, and the doorman. These are the visible tip of the hotel staff, something rather the size of a submarine's periscope peeping above the water in relation to the bulk of the unseen vessel itself. The hundreds of staff whose jobs are 'back of house' as the saying goes in the hotel business are, however, also the people who make the hotel run as it should.

First light

At seven o'clock in the morning — any morning of the 365 in the year — while some of the guests are thinking about getting up or are being aroused by their wake-up calls, certain departments of the hotel have been buzzing with activity for some time already. During the night, amahs who come on duty at midnight have been cleaning the lobby, the Clipper Lounge, and the Coffee Shop. They go off at 6 a.m. and are replaced by the day amahs at 7 a.m., whose job it is to clean various bar areas before eleven when they open.

The four or five reception night-shift staff, who have been coping with much that cannot be done during the day because of the pressure of urgent work as guests check in and out, are in their last hour before being relieved. Such things as telexes are no respecters of the night and arrive 24 hours out of the 24, demanding reservations, cancelling them, changing them. Each has to be dealt with in terms of availability of the requested type of room, and complicated rearrangements have often to be made.

By 7 a.m. the overnight shift of two housekeepers and three roomboys has handed over to the incoming team of roomboys who work a split shift from 7:30 a.m. to 11:30 a.m. then go home, and return at 6 p.m. until 10 p.m. While the overnight room staff work from an office with a wall of red lights which summon them to this or that room anywhere in the hotel, the day shifts work on their assigned floors. Precisely at 7 a.m. two housekeepers arrive and divide the house (as the terminology has it) into upper and lower floors — and some days of the week (which are not stated in advance) one of them comes in early just to check that everything is as it should be.

Since the hotel has a 24-hour room service facility there are cooks for this duty on all night. While there are perhaps only 30 or 40 orders after midnight, there is plenty of work to be done in preparing trays and trolleys for room-service breakfasts, with every detail of what is on them correct and checked. While the trays are stacked on racks in the kitchen, the trolleys present quite another problem. Because of size, only about 20 are stored in the kitchen and the others are sent up, prepared and covered over, to the service areas on each floor.

By seven in the morning these overnight men have been long been relieved by their colleagues, at between 5:30 and 6 a.m. in fact, who then take over the squeezing of the orange juice, the preparing of the bread for toast, the setting out of the eggs. And yet others have arrived in the main kitchen which looks after buffet breakfasts, and breakfasts in the Grill and the Coffee Shop.

Throughout the night, the bakery's 24-hour operation has been continuing with the making of various breads, croissants, Danish pastries; and at seven the bakers are joined by others who make desserts for all the food outlets. They begin making the mousses, the cakes, the French pastries, and all the other sweet things on every restaurant menu.

Breakfast

From seven in the morning until nine or so, the whole room-service operation is a whirl of controlled activity. More precisely than at any other meal time, each breakfast order must reach the guest on time if his or her morning schedule is not to be upset. And considering the number and variety breakfasts ordered, the smooth running of the whole operation is a complex one. The problem of getting the trolleys to the right places is but one of the headaches. It takes one man feeding and minding the hugh toast-maker with its continuously revolving grids to cope with the demand.

Down in the basement the night shift of engineers are in their last hour at seven o'clock. Their night has been spent checking the complex machinery and electrical gadgetry that keep the airconditioning running, the chilled water on tap in every bathroom sterilized ˏand at the correct temperature, among a host of apparatus checks requiring regular visits to several areas spreading from the roof to the basement.

By 8 a.m. when many guests have finished breakfast and some are even checking out for early planes, another phase of activity begins. The clerks in the office behind the reception desk come on and are engulfed in the business of the day. The day-shift reception clerks arrive. The night telephone operators, who are men, are relieved by four women telephonists at 8 a.m. And for them, like everyone else, the next two hours or more are often the busiest time of the day, when most guests make or check the day's arrangements.

Communications

But in fact the telephone room is almost continuously busy — Hong Kong being the banking and business centre it is, and the major banking and business centres of the world being in differing time zones, there is every likelihood that incoming and outgoing calls will take place at almost any hour of the day or night. By this time the night shift have probably done most of the wake-up calls already, but the rest are now started, and the tape with the charming voice of the public relations manager automatically arouses the guests at the right time. Other duties of the telephonists are to attend to a loudspeaker which is connected to microphones in all lifts so that anyone with whatever problem in any of them can be heard, located, and attended to. And there is another piece of equipment which automatically warns of fire, and locates it immediately so that action can be taken.

At precisely 8 a.m. the general manager descends to see the duty manager and the night manager, the latter just about to leave. At that time, on some Saturdays when the Air India early flight has brought the first guests, he may have the chance to greet them in person.

Keeping cool

The chief engineer comes in at eight and begins his personal walkabout, looking at projects in hand and at things to be done during the day. This takes him from the roof to the basement where his office is, and where he inspects the airconditioning plant and the boiler rooms. He, like the general manager one floor up at the same time, inspects the book with comments on all engineering matters kept by the duty engineer, and then starts planning his own morning meetings.

Some idea of the complexity of the unseen machinery over which he has control may be had from a few figures. There are 4 chillers (making cold air for airconditioning), 3 air-handling units (the means by which chilled air is circulated) in the basement, 7 on the roof, a total of 16 major ones elsewhere. The total number of units in the cooling system is about 1,000. To get chilled water that is on tap in every bedroom actually on tap, sterilized by infra-red rays, chilled, circulated in such a way that it is actually cold at the outlet, is one other minor responsibility of the engineer. He has a staff of 63 whose capabilities range from furniture repair and re-upholstering to wiring and expert painting; not to mention others in more strictly engineering jobs.

*George Chinnery, misogynist painter, the only major Western
artist to record the 19th century scene in Macau, Hong Kong, and
South China, has a bar dedicated to his memory*

A walk round the basement where the roar of great pumps vies with the whine of generators along the corridors, brings you suddenly to part of the hotel's wine cellar — a place of quiet where the racks contain everything from Campari and Fernet Branca to champagnes and some of the great vintages in burgundies and clarets. And then back again to the walls of dials and gauges flickering and twitching, and telling the initiates of these mysteries the secrets of systems that keep The Mandarin physically happy.

By now the clerks of the reception office are preparing the lists of arrivals for the day and allocating rooms and suites with information on any special guests — lists which must be ready for the general manager's meeting at 9:15 a.m. The Mandarin has a guest history card for each of its guests in which many particulars are noted — preferences for room or suite, type of business, dates of former stays in the hotel, and other information. Each incoming guest who has such a card on file can be sure that preferences in any matter the hotel has been able to detect will be met if possible. But the work of achieving this service is considerable. The office where this goes on is in a continuing state of turmoil, largely because virtually eighty percent of its activities have to be done at the last moment, while people are checking out in numbers.

Another function of this office is to receive from the housekeeping department news of each room vacated and ready for use. The flurry of activity that begins between eight and nine in the housekeeping department is astonishing to watch. The problems come when there are many early arrivals and many late check-outs. Obviously there must come times when its looks all but impossible to make ready the requisite number of rooms in time for the arrival of the next guests. At 9 a.m. a back-up team of roomboys and house-men (who clean the bathrooms) comes on duty, and rooms are cleaned as swiftly as a highly trained, perfectionist staff can do so.

All change

Simultaneously, the laundry is another hive of industry before nine o'clock. Because rooms are being stripped of their linen and bathrooms of their towels and bathrobes, breakfast trays and trolleys, and breakfast tables in restaurants are yielding up their napery, soiled linen in quantities is arriving. The laundering of such material is contracted out and the first batch leaves around 8:30 a.m. But at the same time clean bedroom and bathroom linen and towels have to be taken to each floor, where it is not possible for space reasons to store enough to keep up with the requirements. So the laundry is one of the most concentrated areas of bustle all morning.

This, however, is by no means the extent of the laundry's activities. At about the same time the guests' laundry is arriving in bags, to-gether with clothes for cleaning and pressing. The dry cleaning is sent out, which sounds as though that is that. But in fact every item has to be tagged. This tagging also applies to each garment, from a sock to a shirt or a blouse, to be washed in the hotel's selection of machines. One man's job is to apply a number to each garment and the same number to the laundry form of that guest. One woman's job is hand washing cuffs and collars before shirts

go into the washing machines.

In another part of the laundry the pressing is done, and a tailor sits behind a mountain of garments, altering or repairing staff uniforms, while in another room seamstresses are replacing lost buttons, doing minor repairs for guests and to bedcovers, curtains, bathrobes.

The executive housekeeper has her own staff meeting each morning at nine, during which she forms a more or less complete pic-ture of what is going on in the whole range of housekeeping activities — everything from some hiccup in the delivery of clean sheets to requests for attention to the flushing in a bathroom. By 9:30 she begins her own rounds. But there are continual messages coming into her department from reception. Can such-and-such a room be got ready quickly since an arriving guest likes that parti-cular one? Mr. X is arriving soon and has ask-ed for extra pillows. Mr. and Mrs. Y will arrive shortly and they have stored baggage — can this be placed ready in the right room?

By ten, the executive housekeeper is attending the general manager's meeting, and after that continues her rounds until lunch.

Critical moments

On balance, as the morning goes on, the hotel empties. But there is a continual stream of arrivals. It is the critical balance of arrivals and departures that occupies much of the time of reception and housekeeping.

At this time the chief engineer attends the daily meeting, but before he ascends to the executive offices he finds time to telephone the several contractors who have men at work in the hotel. By eleven he is back and calls in his supervisors and assistants, and the

In keeping with current taste and trends, The Mandarin suite has been redesigned several times since the hotel opened. The recent concept achieves a subtle balance of East and West

numerous pieces of work that have to be done are arranged and checked with other departments to see that timing is suitable.

The restaurants

The Mandarin has three principal restaurants: The Grill, The Man Wah which serves Chinese food exclusively, and Pierrot, serving speciality French food. There are also the Coffee Shop and the Clipper Lounge — another two food outlets — and at lunchtime the Captain's Bar off the lobby serves food, and the Chinnery Bar upstairs serves what you might expect to find in a fine English pub. The Harlequin Bar with its view, and atmosphere of *grand luxe,* the area through which patrons of Pierrot pass on their way in and out of that superbly elegant restaurant, is

the sole bar not serving food.

All those places must obviously be backed up by kitchens. Pierrot is served from its own kitchen where the waiters come silently in with the orders to the area known as the *passe*. Here, these orders are passed on to the chefs and all others concerned by means of a microphone and speaker system. Since the language of food is French and the language of all the chefs apart from the head chef is Cantonese, it is essential that whoever stands at the *passe* speaks both languages.

A long, white-cloth-covered shelf runs for several yards up to the *passe*, under it a heated cupboard where the dishes are kept. Here the waiters slide their trays along. The one at the head of the line gets his tray furnished with whatever was ordered, as it sits under the infra-red heating lamps that dangle down over the area; and then off he goes, his ankle-length white apron rustling with starch in the approved manner of great French restaurants. The Pierrot restaurant's kitchen is comparatively quiet.

The main kitchen which serves the Grill, and banqueting food in the Connaught and other function rooms, and which makes all the pre-prepared food, is much larger and much noisier. The large menu of the Grill and the variety of dishes to be prepared make this a very busy kitchen.

By about 10 a.m. the main kitchen staff have arrived, preceded a little by the *entremetier* whose job it is to prepare soups and vegetables, and the kitchen is jostling with activity. The one man who preserves his cool and sits quietly in a corner is an oldish Chinese who is an outside contractor supplying the prawns. He sits on a low stool all by himself calmly removing the shells from his wares. All else is hasty but orderly activity directed to producing luncheon for the patrons of the Grill, which is something of an institution in Central and invariably filled with business people. The contrast between the agitation of the kitchen and its gleaming metal surfaces, the heat and savoury smells of food, with the softly lighted elegance of Don Ashton's decor, could hardly be more acute. It is not, however, one that many diners are likely to experience. Little do they imagine how complicated a thing it is to place in front of every one them precisely what was ordered, in perfect condition, with the swift and quiet efficiency expected.

Up on The Mandarin's top floor, at the other end of that area from Pierrot and the Harlequin Bar, is The Man Wah Chinese restaurant, elegant with pink table linen and fine antique Chinese screens. All the tables are round, as they must be in order to eat Chinese food in traditional style. The atmosphere is quite different from that of other restaurants in The Mandarin. When you serve Chinese *haute cuisine* there is a subtle difference from serving fine Western food. The idea behind eating Chinese food (aside from the basic question of nourishment), is as unlike that behind the philosophy of Western meals as is Chinese painting aesthetic from traditional Western art principles.

Chinese kitchens, such as that of Man Wah restaurant, likewise differ widely from their Western equivalents. There are some Chinese dishes that require complicated cooking procedures, but not many. In general, the preparation is what takes the most time, the actual cooking the least. While some Western dishes require sudden big heat to cook, they are on the whole few. In Chinese cuisine it might perhaps be said that the majority of dishes are cooked fast at high temperarture. These are generalisations, but their truth is obvious when the kitchens of the Grill Room and the Man Wah restaurants are compared.

Chinese kitchen

Different food and differing approaches to a meal make the kitchen of the Man Wah unique in the hotel. The whole process of producing the dishes is rather different, entailing much more detailed and prolonged preparation of the raw material. The *passe* operates in a different manner. The traditional rules of Chinese food arrangement make dishes quite as handsome to the eye as

*Evening in the Harlequin Bar — soft lights
and a Hong Kong panorama from the windows*

Western, but subtly other in style (again the analogy of Chinese and Western painting comes to mind). A strange, tall, metal object stands in one corner of the kitchen, slightly resembling some primitive rocket that a Tang Chinese might have fabricated for possible moon-shots. This is the oven in which the Peking duck is suspended — suitably anointed and tended and basted and cossetted — for the cooking process that produces those mouth-watering slivers of duck skin to be wrapped with the Chinese equivalent of chives, and a jam-like red confection, in the finest pancakes of an all but web-like texture.

The scene in the Chinese kitchen, the intense noise as everyone shouts every statement or request, the clanging of the *wok chai* (metal spatulae) on the hugh metal *woks* (deep saucer-shaped steel pans) on the roaring gas flames that give the necessary intense heat,

make the Man Wah kitchen a kind of on-going battle of wits, words, and culinary skills. The results are, surprisingly, the most delicate and succulent of flavours, the most interesting of textures. The Chinese, who evolved over several thousand years one of the two great gastronomic civilizations of the world, put together a process which is basically much more simple in the actual cooking than their only rivals, the French, and achieved a variety of results no less subtle, no less brilliant, and quite as numerous as the French.

Noon

The crescendo of activity in the hotel reaches its peak as guests arrive for pre-luncheon drinks in the bars, and as the clock turns to 12:30 and to 1 p.m.

The analogy with the theatre is inescapable. Everyone is there, on cue. The actors

Dining in Pierrot

are made up, the set is prepared, the lighting plan is gone through, the call boys are at the ready, the stage hands are prepared, the dressers are waiting the next change, the director and the prompter stand in the wings. And, as the clock approaches (in the case of The Mandarin at luncheon) half-past noon, the curtain goes up on a small trickle of action that increases dramatically as minutes pass. And by one o'clock the story is beginning to be narrated, the luncheons served and the conversation animated. There is nothing like the play, or a fine meal finely served, to highlight the art of living, the finesse of business, or the progress of love. Meals are the punctuation of the day, sensuous intervals in the strivings, the serious application of working hours.

The Coffee Shop is full by 12 o'clock or a little after, and a line begins to form in the south entry of the hotel for places as they become vacant. The Captain's Bar has filled up with its habitués; and the Chinnery Bar on the same floor as the Grill has its own faithful clientele who like the pub atmosphere.

As for the Clipper Lounge, the gold figure of Justice, cannot survey but, we may imagine, can at least hear the increasing buzz of conversation as the comfortable armchairs fill with both regular local people and a scattering of hotel guests just in from shopping.

The Clipper Lounge has its own compact kitchen, making for rapid service. Its regular luncheon buffet presents an array of food that can hardly fail to please. The buffet has of course been set up during the morning on immaculate white linen-covered tables against the black marble of the wall behind it, and furnished just before lunch.

Visible from parts of the Clipper Lounge is

the thronged lobby with, from time to time, the general manager talking to a guest between his visits to all the restaurants during luncheon. And in every public area of the hotel there is an atmosphere of relaxation, yet of a multitude of things going on, which continues until at least two in the afternoon. Then, perceptibly, the activity begins to wind down and there are very many more people coming down in lifts, than going up; emerging from bars and restaurants and leaving for the world outside, than there are entering. By three the play is almost over, the last of the action done.

In the kitchens as the final orders are filled, the cooks begin to leave for their afternoon break. The pot washers and dish washers are the busiest people there, and stewards who clean the kitchens. As the covers are removed, the laundry reels from another onslaught of linen.

Afternoon

The kitchens are quiet except for the chefs on duty in the cold kitchen preparing the canapes for a reception, sometimes even two or three functions, starting at 5:30 or later. Staff are setting up the tables and the flowers in function rooms; and the national flags, if one of the receptions is the celebration of the national day of some country represented in Hong Kong.

The storekeeper may be finding the requisite number of big silver punch bowls for some party, and the keeper of the ready-use liquor stockroom is probably getting requests for fresh supplies from the bars.

In offices the heads of departments try to get down to paperwork, and the morning shift of telephonists gives way at 3:30 to the next who will stay until 11 p.m. when the men for the overnight duty arrive. The engineering shift changes at 4 p.m. when a fresh lot takes over until midnight. Then the night shift arrives. The reception desk staff also go off at 4 p.m. and a new shift works until midnight, but the staff in the office who arrived at eight in the morning leave for good at 6 p.m. The same sort of programme applies to the staff on the enquiry desk, and the men in the baggage office.

The executive housekeeper, of an afternoon, finds herself with a many a task. It may be that she has to make the calculations that will clinch a decision whether to order new linen before the situation arises in which there would not be sufficient for replacement. All the sheets and pillowcases come from Ireland, home of the finest in linen. So, too, does the table linen. The delivery time is long, thus linen must be ordered in November to arrive by April-May of the following year. Items such as towels — those most luxuriant thick soft enveloping towels of The Mandarin — are ordered locally and specially made.

For the guest it is natural to accept that the bathroom contains excellent soap, and an offering of shampoo, foam bath, and eau de toilette in a handy package, together with shower cap and other things he and she may not have brought. They find, too, a folder in the bedroom with writing paper (personalised in many cases), luggage stickers, postcards, information leaflets, note pads, and a pen. It is convenient, too, that small bars are in the rooms and suites. But in terms of the organisation required to furnish all these items on a daily and regular basis, and in terms of ordering, it means quite considerable effort in the housekeeping office.

Evening

As afternoon turns to early evening the character of the hotel gently changes. Daylight fades. The internal lighting takes over. The balance of emphasis changes in the lobby, the gold Chinese carvings, the coffee-onyx wall becoming richer, shadows collecting here and there. The musicians in the Clipper Lounge who have been playing for a couple of hours now cease, the teatime crowd there makes its way out and is replaced by the drink-after-work and then drink-before-dinner guests. People arrive in the lobby, meeting friends before going out to dinner, or for drinks and dinner in The Mandarin itself.

The waiters are putting the finishing touches to tables in the restaurants, the first of the receptions is begining in the Connaught Rooms, and a flood of cars and taxis brings back visiting executives from work and the tourists from their various ploys. The bars are getting livelier and the general manager is probably in the lobby to have a word with whomever passes through.

Soon, after the guests have dressed and left for dinner, the roomboys will be turning down beds, emptying ashtrays and waste baskets, replacing used towels and setting the breakfast order tags in convenient places to be completed and hung outside before guests retire.

At the top of the hotel the Harlequin Bar is filling up, its dark green and auburn discreetly lit, serving to focus attention on the view of the sparkle of Hong Kong and its harbour as night claims them. Whatever unkind remarks are made about Hong Kong's newer tall buildings in daytime, the evening, the night, those great softeners of the day's blemishes, make them all into towers of light on a carpet of neon laid on the brink of the dark water of the harbour, across which more lights scurry on errands apparently as secret as night itself.

By eight or so, Pierrot is filling up, diners passing in by Picasso's 1929 painting of his son Paul dressed in pierrot costume: in to the warm reds and the gold of the restaurant that are so flattering to women, so entirely comfortable to be in.

Famous chefs

Pierrot, like the Grill, from time to time entertains as guest chef one or other of the world's renowned masters of the art. Now and then there is no need to go to Tours in France, for M. Barrier himself is in Pierrot's kitchen, and his supreme food is being served by waiters every bit as versed in their jobs as those of Tours: or Louis Outhier from l'Oasis at La Napoule, or Michel Troisgros of Les Frères Troisgros at Roanne in the Loire, or Marc Haeberlin from L'Auberge de l'Ill, add their particular brilliance to the restaurant.

From each of them The Mandarin chefs learn a little more, each leaves a legacy of a recipe of two which enter the repertoire of Pierrot or The Grill. Prue Leith from London is the greatest expert on British food (something many people were suprised to find existed!), and her three weeks at The Grill were enthusiastically received, the Chinese cooks marvelling at the simplicity of the cooking method in comparison to that of much French food.

Palace food and lacquer screen in the Man Wah restaurant

Similarly, the Man Wah restaurant has had a team of Chinese cooks from China itself. And the Coffee Shop enjoyed the curries of Percy Sullivan, as did the Clipper Lounge at luncheon.

By nine or so, diners in the Grill are making their choices in an elegant environment among whose features is a design that permits the feeling for each table's occupants of a certain privacy without being cut off from the rest of the room. Dinner there is more leisurely than lunch, and the atmosphere fosters the feeling that there's a whole long evening to enjoy food and conversation and the wines that have for so long been evolving to perfection in Europe, as their accompaniment.

The Man Wah restaurant at night is one of the few Chinese restaurants where the finest food can be enjoyed in reasonably quiet surroundings. The tendency in Chinese restaurants is to a level of decibels produced by the diners themselves which precludes conversation not at the level of a shout — enjoyable but in the end slightly fatiguing. Impeccable service, intelligent help with food unfamiliar to the non-Chinese diner, coupled with banquet-style dishes, make the Man Wah highly popular. To eat there is certainly not the same experience as it would be in a crowded Chinese restaurant a mile along the road in Wanchai where splendid food can also be found, but where the chances are that several clattering games of mahjong will be emitting a machinegun volley and players and diners will perforce shout to be heard at all. The Man Wah is the palace of Chinese restau-

And so to bed

rants — but not at all stiff.

And so the evening matures in the several restaurants and bars of The Mandarin. The day's urgencies and preoccupations fade from the thoughts of guests as they relax. A great hotel is like one of those great houses of yesteryear, those mansions in town or country in the days when they still existed and were lived in and run and loved as their owners intended them to be. There, too, dinner proceeded as one of the day's expected, relaxing social occasions, as well as being a gastronomic event during which time passed pleasingly and life's cares were relinquished awhile in favour of its human and culinary delights.

As the guests make their way to bed, the day done, The Mandarin mansion, like those of former days but with large additions of services and facilities, continues, back of house, into the night's essential occupations. Late returning guests from parties and dinners elsewhere may probably encounter an amah with duster emerging from the Grotto in the gold and onyx lobby wall. They pick up their keys and messages from still smiling staff, and are shepherded to the lifts by the pageboys.

But, then and later, in places they have never seen, the trolleys and trays are being set for breakfast, the orange and grapefruit juices are being assiduously squeezed, and the bakers are at work on that fresh selection of breads, rolls, croissants, and Danish pastries for their breakfast in a few hours time.

The Best Hotel in the World

In April 1984 the readers of the business travel magazine Executive Travel, published in London, voted The Mandarin the best hotel in the world.

Arriving as this accolade did in the hotel's twenty-first year, before the celebrations to mark its coming of age, the choice of The Mandarin was a particularly fitting honour greatly valued by all members of the staff, and of course by Mandarin International Hotels Ltd

*Night has fallen. The lights of Hong Kong
keep the sky bright. The Supreme Court, domed
and turreted, forms the foreground, and The
Mandarin rises full of light between The
Connaught Centre's thousand eyes at the right and
the throng of offices on the landward side*

ISBN 962-7480-01-0